· THE SCHOOLS HISTORY PROJECT ·
S·H·P
· OFFICIAL TEXT ·

BRITAIN & THE GREAT WAR

REVISED EDITION FOR GCSE

a study in depth

DISCOVERING THE PAST FOR GCSE

Greg Hetherton

Series Editor: Colin Shephard

HODDER
EDUCATION
AN HACHETTE UK COMPANY

Acknowledgements

With thanks to Peter Mantin and Terry Fiehn for ideas and material used in this revised edition

Photographs reproduced by kind permission of:
cover Imperial War Museum, London. **p.4** The Illustrated London News Picture Library. **p.5** *both* The Hulton-Getty Collection. **p.6** *top* Michael Holford; *bottom* Greater London Photograph Library. **p.7** *top left* Topham; *top right* The Illustrated London News Picture Library; *centre left and right* Mary Evans Picture Library; *bottom* Reproduced by permission of *Punch*. **p.8** *top centre and centre* The Hulton-Getty Collection; *bottom left* Topham; *bottom right* Beamish, The North of England Open Air Museum, Co. Durham. **p.9** *both* The Hulton-Getty Collection. **p.10** *all* Mary Evans Picture Library; **p.11** *top* Mary Evans Picture Library, *bottom* The Hulton Getty Collection; **p.20** *all* Imperial War Museum, London. **p.21** *centre* and *left* Imperial War Museum, London; *bottom* The Illustrated London News Picture Library. **p.22** Peter Newark's Historical Pictures. **p.23** *both*. **pp.26–27** *all*. **p.29** *top* Imperial War Museum, London. **p.30** *top* National Museum of Labour History. **p.30** *centre* and *bottom*, **p.36** *all*, **p.37** *bottom* Imperial War Museum, London. **p.37** *top* Tate Gallery, London. **p.40** Imperial War Museum, London. **p.41** Copyright © BBC. **p.43** Imperial War Museum, London. **p.44** Reproduced by permission of *Punch*. **p.46** *top* Imperial War Museum, London, *bottom* Ben Walsh; **pp.47–48** *all* Imperial War Museum, London; **p.49** The Tank Museum; **pp.50–51** *all* Imperial War Museum, London; **p.52** *top* right Ben Walsh; **p.52** *rest* Imperial War Museum, London; **pp.54–55** *all* Imperial War Museum, London; **p.57** *top* Imperial War Museum, London, *bottom* Ben Walsh; **pp.61–77** *all* Imperial War Museum, London; **p.78** Popperfoto; **p.79** Süddeutscher Verlag Bilderdienst; **pp.80–81** *all* David King; **p.84** *both* Peter Newark's Historical Pictures. **p.85** *both*, **p.87** *top* Imperial War Museum, London. **p.87** *bottom* Popperfoto. **pp. 88–89** *all*, **p.91** *bottom* Imperial War Museum, London. **p.93** Fitzwilliam Museum, University of Cambridge. **p.94** Frost Historical Newspapers; **p.95** *top* National Museum of Labour History; *bottom* Imperial War Museum, London. **p.96** The Hulton-Getty Collection. **p.97** *top right* John Johnson Collection, Bodleian Library; *rest* Mary Evans Picture Library. **p.98** Mansell Collection. **p.99** Mary Evans Picture Library. **p.101** Southampton City Heritage (Oral Heritage). **p.103** *top* Warwickshire County Museum; *bottom* Mary Evans Picture Library. **pp.106–107** *all* Imperial War Museum, London.

© Greg Hetherton 1993, 1998

First published in 1993
by Hodder Education,
an Hachette UK Company
338 Euston Road,
London NW1 3BH

Revised edition 1998

Reprinted 1999, 2001, 2002, 2003, 2004, 2005, 2006, 2007, 2008, 2010, 2011

Layouts by Ann Samuel
Artwork by David Anstey; Art Construction; Phil Ford; Linden Artists; Peter Bull Art Studio; Steve Smith

Typeset in $11\frac{1}{2}/12\frac{1}{2}$ Quorum Book by Wearset, Boldon, Tyne and Wear

Printed in Dubai
A catalogue entry for this title is available from the British Library

ISBN- 978 0 7195 7347 7

Note: The wording and sentence structure of some written sources have been adapted and simplified to make them accessible to all pupils, while faithfully preserving the sense of the original.

The extract from *Blackadder Goes Forth* on p.41 is reproduced by kind permission of Richard Curtis and Ben Elton.

Vera Brittain's poem *To My Brother* from *Testament of Youth* is included with the permission of Paul Berry and Mark Bostridge, her Literary Executors, and Victor Gollancz Ltd.

Extracts from Richard Aldington's poem *Trench Idyll* are reproduced by permission of Rosica Colin Limited. © The Estate of Richard Aldington.

Poems and prose by Siegfried Sassoon are reproduced by permission of George Sassoon.

Extracts from *The Bumper Biggles Book* and *Biggles, Pioneer Air Fighter* are reproduced by permission of A.P. Watt Ltd on behalf of W.E. Johns (Publications) Ltd.

Every effort has been made to trace all the copyright holders, but if any have been inadvertently overlooked the publishers will be pleased to make the necessary arrangement at the first opportunity.

The Schools History Project

Set up in 1972 to bring new life to history for students aged 13–16, the Schools History Project continues to play an innovatory role in secondary history education. From the start, SHP aimed to show how good history has an important contribution to make to the education of a young person. It does this by creating courses and materials which both respect the importance of up-to-date, well-researched history and provide enjoyable learning experiences for students.

Since 1978 the Project has been based at Trinity and All Saints University College Leeds. It continues to support, inspire and challenge teachers through the annual conference, regional courses and website: http://www.schoolshistoryproject.org.uk. The Project is also closely involved with government bodies and awarding bodies in the planning of courses for Key Stage 3, GCSE and A level.

Series consultants
Terry Fiehn
Tim Lomas
Martin and Jenny Tucker

Words printed in SMALL CAPITALS are defined in the Glossary on page 110.

Contents

Edwardian Britain: the Golden Age?

IN 1901 Queen Victoria died. The period between her death and the outbreak of the Great War in 1914 is known as the Edwardian period. It was seen by many people at the time, and by historians since, as a 'golden age'. It was as if the sun always shone and everyone was having a good time. It was the perfect time to be alive. Some historians believe that all this was destroyed for ever by the Great War, or the First World War as it is now called.

This book will help you to decide:
- whether the time before the Great War was a golden age for everybody
- whether the War destroyed this golden age and made everyone's lives worse
- whether things would have changed anyway even without the War.

The Edwardian period

Edward VII became king in 1901. He was nearly 60 years old, and had waited a long time to become king. During that time he lived a very different life from that of his mother, Queen Victoria. He loved having a good time. He gambled and hunted and loved horse racing: his horses won the Derby three times and the Grand National once. He surrounded himself with the most beautiful women of the time, and had affairs with several actresses.

SOURCE 1 The future King Edward VII leading his horse into the winner's enclosure at the 1896 Derby

Between 1903 and 1913 the amount ► spent by local councils on children's education increased from £10 million to over £30 million

◄ **1906** Workman's Compensation Act. A worker who was injured by an accident at work or caught a disease at work could claim compensation

1908 Old Age Pensions introduced: ► five shillings a week for people over 70 with an income of less that £21 a year

When he finally became king, it was clear that the serious days of Queen Victoria were over. When he was crowned in 1902 he held massive banquets for the poor, which cost over £30,000 – an enormous sum of money in those days. He was a very popular king, and had a big influence on the way many other people led their lives.

For the rich – the upper class and the middle class – it was a time of great comfort and luxury. They lived in comfortable houses with large gardens. Many of them had so much money they did not need to work. But they had a busy time watching polo at Ranelagh, horse racing at Ascot or yachting at Cowes, going to dinner parties or dances, or watching the opera.

Edward made popular the idea that the weekend was a time for rest and leisure. Many people used the weekends for going to the seaside.

At home the upper and middle classes had servants to do most of their housework and cooking. A whole class of British society grew up never needing to do anything around the house, however simple. These people never had to make a pot of tea, wash up, mend or iron clothes, post a letter, or even brush their own hair or choose their own clothes.

At this time fashions were changing. Houses became lighter than Victorian homes and less cluttered with heavy furniture. White paint and light-coloured wallpaper replaced heavy reds and browns. Glass conservatories became popular.

1911 National Insurance Act. Workers and employers made weekly contributions which were used to give workers sickness benefit and free medical care. In trades like building, where there was a lot of temporary unemployment, unemployment pay was also given

SOURCE 2 Reforms introduced during the Edwardian period

Women's clothing fashions changed as well. They wore dresses that gave them a tiny waist and a full bosom. Some skirts were made so tight round the ankles that only small steps were possible.

Motor cars were beginning to be a common sight on the roads. In London horse-drawn buses were being replaced by petrol-driven buses and trams.

The rich believed in progress. They were sure that their lives were better than their parents' and that things would go on getting better all the time!

Now let's see if the poor had any reason to believe that things were getting better.

Between 1901 and 1914 the measures shown in Source 2 began to give the poor some protection against the worst evils of the Victorian period.

SOURCE 3 A photograph taken in 1912. The family lived in this one room

SOURCE 4 The living room of a skilled worker's house, 1910. This man worked in the engineering industry. There were five rooms in his house

SOURCE 5 Houses in Hampstead Garden Suburb on the outskirts of London. They were built in 1905 to provide cheap housing for all classes of people

SOURCE 6 Providence Place, Stepney, East London, in 1909

SOURCE 7 From an article written in 1913

❝*Mr H. is 22 and works in a brewery. He earns £1 per week. He gives his wife, who is twenty, all of his wage. They have one child of six months.*

His wife used to work in a polish factory, but she was dismissed (and paid a small bonus) when she got married, because the firm does not employ married women. She is an excellent housewife and keeps their one room clean and comfortable . . .❞

SOURCE 8 From a biography of Daisy and Walter Thackrah, written by their son. They rented a house in Hampstead Garden Suburb (see Source 5)

❝*Spring 1914 was a beautiful time for them both. Things grew and budded in the garden . . . They walked through the two woods in the road and across the fields all around them . . .*

Daisy sang at her housework, which was soon done in the morning. She needed only to go to the shops once or twice a week. She was a little bored in the afternoons except for the tea parties with the neighbours, and she looked forward impatiently to Walter's return, which was so often late in the evening. It would be all right when she had a family . . .❞

SOURCE 9 A middle-class woman describes moving into her new house in 1900

❝*We modernised it with a service lift [to bring food and water upstairs from the kitchen in the basement], electric light and a telephone.*

The house contained a large basement, three sitting rooms, a lounge–hall and seven bedrooms. All the rooms were warmed by coal fires, there were nursery meals to be carried up and down, hot water to be taken to the bedrooms, and we entertained a great deal. Yet we found little difficulty of running the house with a staff of a nurse, a parlour maid, a housemaid and a cook. Later we kept a manservant for £70 a year. The cook earned £28. The nurse's salary was £40.❞

SOURCE 10 From a survey by Seebohm Rowntree in York in 1901. He calculated that a family of two adults and three children could just live on 21s 8d a week. Nearly half the workers in the country earned less than 20s a week

❝*[To manage on 21s 8d] . . . they must never spend a penny on a railway or bus fare. They must never purchase a half penny newspaper. The children must have no pocket money for dolls, marbles or sweets. The father must smoke no tobacco, and must drink no beer. The mother must never buy pretty clothes for herself or for her children. Finally, the wage-earner must never be absent from his work for a single day.*❞

SOURCE 11 Children at the seaside in 1909

SOURCE 14 People drinking tea outside the clubhouse at Ranelagh, painted in 1907

SOURCE 12 Ladies' fashions in 1914

SOURCE 13 'A Quiet Sunday in Our Village' from *Punch*, 6 June 1906

1. Which of Sources 1–14 show or describe
   ■ poor working-class families who lived hard lives
   ■ very rich families who lived comfortable lives?
   Give reasons for all your choices.
2. Are there any sources you have not included in your answer to question 1? What type of people do these show?
3. What hardships did poor working-class families have to face in their daily lives? Support your answers with evidence from the sources.
4. Make a list of the differences you can find between the lives of the rich and the lives of the poor.
5. What does the role of women seem to be?
6. From the evidence in these sources write an essay entitled 'Was the period 1901–1914 a golden age?'

7

Was the Golden Age coming to an end?

FOR 150 years Britain's trade and industry had been growing quickly. Middle-class owners and managers had made a lot of money out of industry. Some skilled workers had also done well – their wages were good, they could afford small but respectable houses, and they were proud of their position in society.

However, in the large industrial towns, such as London, Leeds and Manchester, many men, women and children as young as ten worked as unskilled labourers in factories. The conditions were often dangerous. The wages were low and the hours were long. The same problems were faced by miners and by labourers in the countryside.

Work was divided into 'women's jobs' and 'men's jobs'. It was assumed that women could only do light, indoor work which did not need strength or skill. Women were usually paid less than men, even though they worked the same hours. Thirteen million men had paid jobs, but only five and a half million women. Many married women worked at home, either as housewives or making clothes or doing laundry for desperately low wages in the room where they lived, ate and slept.

An alternative to this for a young, unmarried girl was to work as a domestic servant. In domestic work pay was low, a fifteen- to sixteen-hour day was quite normal and there was hardly any free time, even at weekends.

Source 1 shows you the kind of work women were doing outside their homes in 1914.

> **1.** Can you think of any jobs today that are usually regarded as 'men's' or 'women's' jobs? Why is this?

Percentage of workforce

| | 0 | 10 | 20 | 30 | 40 | 50 | 60 | 70 | 80 | 90 | 100 | |

Domestic service
Textiles/clothing
Food/drink/tobacco
Transport
Manufacturing/engineering
Farming/forestry
Mining/quarrying/building

Total workforce

Key

■ Women   ■ Men

▲**SOURCE 1** Percentages of men and women workers in various industries in 1914

▼**SOURCE 2** A hat factory in Manchester, 1909

▲**SOURCE 4** Women telephone switchboard operators

SOURCE 3 Women haymaking

SOURCE 5 A reconstruction of a Co-op shop in 1913

2. From the evidence on page 8 make a list of jobs that were done mainly by women, jobs done mainly by men and jobs done by either.
3. Women were not allowed to work down mines, but young boys were. What does this tell you about attitudes at this time?

Protests on the eve of war

Even before the Great War broke out in 1914, there were signs that the Golden Age was coming to an end.

In the years before the War, the poor became even worse off. More people were unemployed. Those who had jobs found that although prices were going up their wages were not. The dockers were still being paid the 'dockers' tanner' (6d an hour) they had fought for in 1889! More and more workers joined trade unions to get their pay and working conditions improved.

The poor found their living conditions hard to bear because they could see that the rich were still living a life of luxury. Some union leaders called for all the unions to join together in a massive strike. This would bring both industry and the government to their knees and the unions could then take over the running of the country. Many workers did not want to go as far as this, but from 1910 until 1914 strikes broke out in all parts of the country. Many of them were very violent.

SOURCE 6 London policemen marching into Tonypandy in South Wales in 1910. They later clashed with striking miners

SOURCE 7 A photograph taken in 1912, when London was running out of food due to a transport strike. Police are escorting this meat van into London

The leading strikers were the railwaymen, the dockers and the miners. The government called in new workers to replace the strikers and used troops to protect these workers. The troops even did some jobs, such as running the trains.

In 1911 one million workers went on strike. In 1913 the three big unions, the railwaymen, the transport workers and the miners, formed an alliance to organise a general strike of all workers. Some historians believe the government would have been defeated by these powerful unions if the War had not broken out.

SOURCE 8 From a book by G. Dangerfield called *The Strange Death of Liberal England*, written in 1937. Here he is describing the effects of the dockers' strike in 1912

66 *Everything began to die – coal and water services, gas and electricity, railway, road and river transport. As for the butter trade, the Danish butter came in casks and was not refrigerated; it was growing rancid in the mounting heat. The frozen meat from Argentina and New Zealand – on which London depended – was going bad. Famine drew nearer by the hour.* 99

Another group posed a threat to law and order during this period: women. You might expect that poor women suffering from appalling living and working conditions would cause trouble for the government, but in fact the leaders of the protesters were often rich, well-educated women. They were protesting because they wanted the right to vote in elections.

Many women believed that unless they were given the right to vote they would not be able to improve their living and working conditions. The Women's Social and Political Union (WSPU) was formed in 1903 to try and persuade the government to give women the vote (SUFFRAGE). It was led by Mrs Emmeline Pankhurst, and its members were known as the SUFFRAGETTES.

SOURCE 9 A speech by Mrs Pankhurst in 1913

66 *It was rapidly becoming clear to my mind that men regarded women as a servant class in the community and that women were going to remain in that class until they lifted themselves out of it. I asked myself many times, what was to be done?* 99

SOURCE 10 Two postcards produced by the Suffragettes

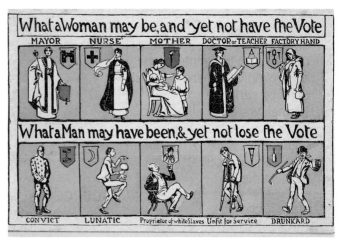

SOURCE 11 A Suffragette postcard of 1910

1. Look back at page 9. What aims did the strikers and the Suffragettes have in common?
2. How did their aims differ?
3. Can you think of any argument that a man might have used to disagree with the comments in Source 11?

It may seem difficult for us today to understand why women were not allowed to vote, but at that time many men thought women could not make sensible decisions, and that politics was a man's business. Even those who supported women's right to vote were worried that, because women outnumbered men, women would have too much influence.

In 1910 the House of Commons voted on whether women should be given the vote. A Bill was actually passed by a large majority of 139. But in November Parliament was dissolved before the measure became law. Women tried to meet the Prime Minister to get him to promise to keep the Bill, but he refused. A violent protest followed – 119 women were arrested and two died from injuries received in the skirmishes.

From 1910 onwards the protests of the women campaigners became increasingly violent. Two distinct groups of women campaigners emerged, the Suffragettes and the Suffragists. The Suffragists were moderates. They held meetings and demonstrations and tried to persuade politicians by argument that women should have the vote.

The Suffragettes became more extreme. They were prepared to break the law in order to get what they wanted. They chained themselves to the railings of MPs' houses, set fire to pillar boxes, attacked policemen, broke shop windows and slashed pictures in the National Gallery. They attacked property, such as 'men only' golf courses. One died when she threw herself at the King's horse during the Derby of 1913.

> **4.** Sources 12–14 illustrate various actions by women campaigners. Which would be approved by the Suffragists? Which by the Suffragettes?

SOURCE 12 From the *Daily Telegraph* newspaper, 2 March 1912

A band of women set out on such a window breaking campaign in the main streets of the West End as London has ever known. For a quarter of an hour, nothing was to be heard in the Strand, Downing Street, Piccadilly and Oxford Street but falling, shattered glass . . . Women who a moment before had appeared to be on peaceful shopping expeditions, produced from their bags hammers, stones and sticks and began an attack on the nearest windows.

SOURCE 13 A peaceful demonstration in 1912

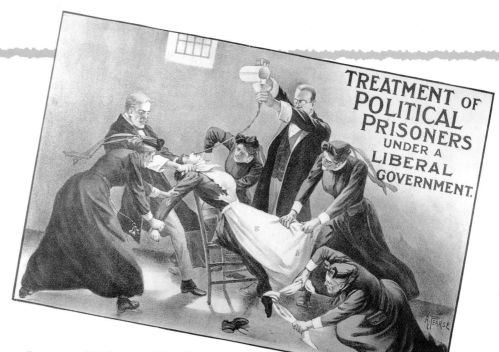

SOURCE 14
A Suffragette poster showing a prisoner being force fed

Between 1912 and 1914 the pressure mounted. The Suffragettes' campaign became more and more violent. They bombed the Chancellor of the Exchequer Lloyd George's newly built house, and set fire to public buildings and property.

The government was determined not to give in to violence. Many Suffragettes were put in prison. Some went on hunger strike. If Suffragettes died in prison they might gain public support, so the government force fed them. In turn, the Suffragettes produced posters such as Source 14 which made this government policy unpopular. So in 1913 the government passed the so-called 'Cat and Mouse Act'. This let women out of prison if their health became bad, but they were arrested again when they had recovered.

In 1910 it had seemed as if women would soon get the vote. But by 1914 it seemed the movement was getting nowhere. The Suffragettes were losing public support because of their violent protests. The government was as determined as ever not to give in to them. Their right to vote seemed as far away as ever.

> **5.** Why do you think the government introduced the 'Cat and Mouse Act'?
> **6.** Using the information on pages 10–11 say whether you think the Suffragettes' campaign had been successful up to 1914.
> **7.** Who were the greater threat to the government, the strikers or the Suffragettes?

> **1.** Put this heading in your book: '1914: Are the good times coming to an end for Britain?'
> Divide your page in half. Head one column 'yes' and write in it evidence that suggests they were. Head the other column 'no' and write in it evidence to suggest they were not.
> Then come to a conclusion, explaining your answer.

Why did war break out in 1914?

Was war expected in Europe?

Source 1 shows Europe in 1914. For a number of years tension between the main European powers had been increasing. Each country had been openly building up its military strength.

In 1914 there were two main power blocks:
- **the Triple Entente:** Great Britain, France and Russia (formed in 1907)
- **the Triple Alliance:** Germany, Italy and Austria–Hungary (formed in 1882).

Each member of the alliances promised to help its allies if they were attacked by a country belonging to the other alliance.

SOURCE 1 Europe in 1914

1. Draw a grid with six columns, one each for Britain, France, Russia, Germany, Austria–Hungary and Italy. Using the information in Source 1, fill in population, number of soldiers, number of warships, overseas empire (tick or cross) and main rivals and friends for each one.
2. Which of the six countries do you think was the strongest in 1914? Give your reasons.
3. Which alliance do you think was stronger?
4. Is there any reason why Germany might want to attack Britain?
5. Do you think that if war broke out between two of these countries, all the other countries would be dragged in as well? Explain your answer.

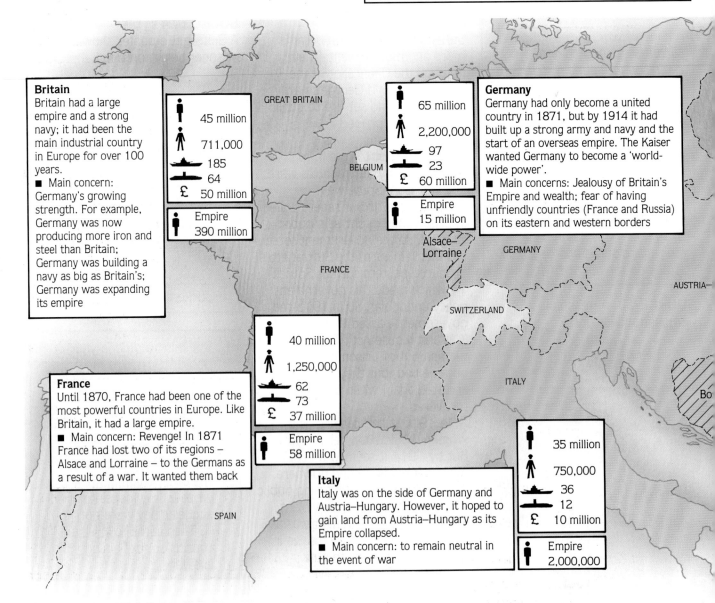

Britain
Britain had a large empire and a strong navy; it had been the main industrial country in Europe for over 100 years.
- Main concern: Germany's growing strength. For example, Germany was now producing more iron and steel than Britain; Germany was building a navy as big as Britain's; Germany was expanding its empire

45 million
711,000
185
64
£ 50 million
Empire 390 million

Germany
Germany had only become a united country in 1871, but by 1914 it had built up a strong army and navy and the start of an overseas empire. The Kaiser wanted Germany to become a 'world-wide power'.
- Main concerns: Jealousy of Britain's Empire and wealth; fear of having unfriendly countries (France and Russia) on its eastern and western borders

65 million
2,200,000
97
23
£ 60 million
Empire 15 million

France
Until 1870, France had been one of the most powerful countries in Europe. Like Britain, it had a large empire.
- Main concern: Revenge! In 1871 France had lost two of its regions – Alsace and Lorraine – to the Germans as a result of a war. It wanted them back

40 million
1,250,000
62
73
£ 37 million
Empire 58 million

Italy
Italy was on the side of Germany and Austria–Hungary. However, it hoped to gain land from Austria–Hungary as its Empire collapsed.
- Main concern: to remain neutral in the event of war

35 million
750,000
36
12
£ 10 million
Empire 2,000,000

Was war expected in Britain?

Under the Triple Entente Britain promised to help France if it was attacked by Germany. Anti-German feeling had been building up in Britain long before 1914. People in many walks of life openly discussed the German threat. By 1914 a German attack on France seemed very likely. People expected that such an attack could trigger off a war in Europe. Sources 2–4 are extracts from the many novels, articles, letters and speeches which dealt with this subject.

SOURCE 2 From the *Daily Mail* newspaper, 1909

❝*Germany is deliberately preparing to destroy the British Empire . . . We are all to be drilled and schooled and uniformed by German officials. Britain alone stands in the way of Germany's path to world power and domination.*❞

SOURCE 3 From *Howards End*, a novel by E.M. Forster, written in 1910

❝*The remark 'England and Germany are bound to fight' makes war a little more likely each time that it is made, and is therefore made more often by the gutter press of each nation*❞

SOURCE 4 From a letter written by David Lloyd George to Winston Churchill in 1911. They were both powerful politicians and future prime ministers

❝*I have been reading the Foreign Office papers. They are full of menace. The thunderclouds are gathering. I am not at all sure that we are prepared or are preparing . . . I am inclined to think that the chances of war are increasing.*❞

1. Source 3 is from a novel. Can it help us to understand whether people in Britain expected war? Explain your answer.
2. Which sources suggest people 'wanted' war?

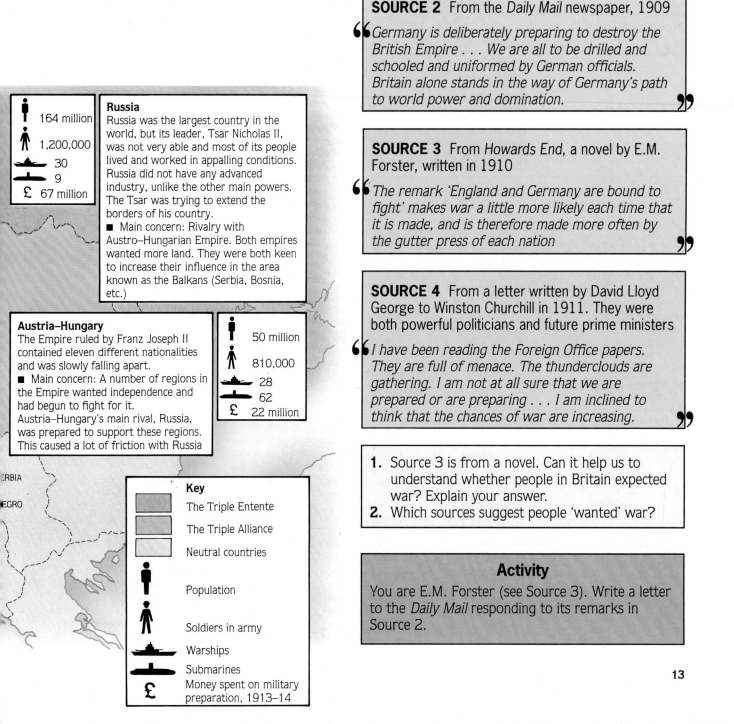

Russia

	164 million
	1,200,000
	30
	9
£	67 million

Russia was the largest country in the world, but its leader, Tsar Nicholas II, was not very able and most of its people lived and worked in appalling conditions. Russia did not have any advanced industry, unlike the other main powers. The Tsar was trying to extend the borders of his country.
■ Main concern: Rivalry with Austro–Hungarian Empire. Both empires wanted more land. They were both keen to increase their influence in the area known as the Balkans (Serbia, Bosnia, etc.)

Austria–Hungary
The Empire ruled by Franz Joseph II contained eleven different nationalities and was slowly falling apart.
■ Main concern: A number of regions in the Empire wanted independence and had begun to fight for it. Austria–Hungary's main rival, Russia, was prepared to support these regions. This caused a lot of friction with Russia

	50 million
	810,000
	28
	62
£	22 million

ERBIA

EGRO

Key
The Triple Entente
The Triple Alliance
Neutral countries

Population

Soldiers in army

Warships

Submarines

£ Money spent on military preparation, 1913–14

Steps to war

BRITAIN was not the only country expecting war. Each European power had made its own plans. Many of their peoples also expected a war. It would take only a small spark to set the guns blazing.

The spark finally came in June 1914. In Sarajevo, in the state of Bosnia, the heir to the Austrian throne was assassinated by a young student, Gavrilo Princip. This set off a chain reaction throughout Europe.

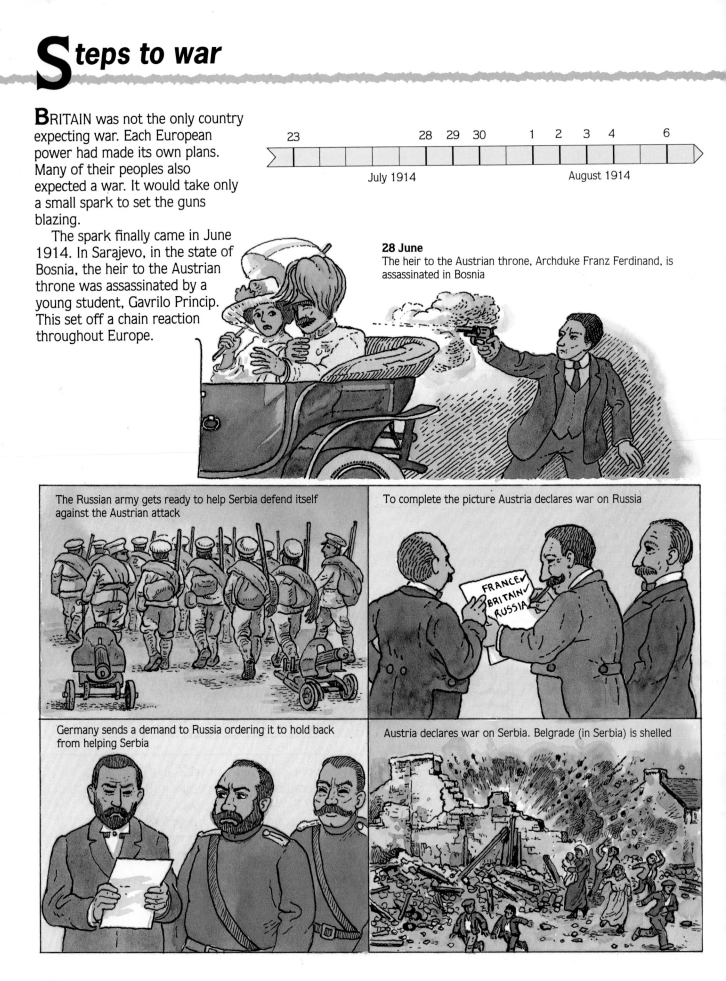

```
  23              28  29  30      1   2   3   4       6
```
July 1914   August 1914

28 June
The heir to the Austrian throne, Archduke Franz Ferdinand, is assassinated in Bosnia

The Russian army gets ready to help Serbia defend itself against the Austrian attack

To complete the picture Austria declares war on Russia

FRANCE
BRITAIN
RUSSIA

Germany sends a demand to Russia ordering it to hold back from helping Serbia

Austria declares war on Serbia. Belgrade (in Serbia) is shelled

Germany declares war on France and invades NEUTRAL Belgium. Britain orders Germany to withdraw from Belgium

BRITISH GOVERNMENT DEMANDS GERMANS LEAVE BELGIUM

The Germans are still in Belgium. Britain declares war on Germany

BRITAIN DECLARES WAR ON GERMANY

Germany declares war on Russia. It also begins to move its army towards France and Belgium

BRITAIN
GERMANY
FRANCE
AUSTRIA-HUNGARY

Austria blames Serbia for the killing of Archduke Ferdinand

It's Serbia that is behind this!

The Serbians trained those Bosnian assassins.

The French army is put on a war footing ready to fight any German invasion

1. The illustrations on these two pages show the events between 28 June and 6 August 1914 that led to war. See if you can put them in order.

2. Divide into groups. From the following list, choose five factors which you think were the most important reasons for war breaking out.
   - Germany's invasion of Belgium
   - the increasing size of the German army and navy
   - the behaviour of Austria towards Serbia
   - Britain's rivalry with Germany
   - France's desire for revenge
   - Germany's fear of being surrounded by France and Russia
   - Austria's rivalry with Russia
   - the size of the British Empire
   - Germany's desire to dominate Europe
   - suspicion between the main powers
   - the assassination of Archduke Ferdinand
   - the alliance system.

   From your top five reasons choose one which is a long-term cause (which built up over time) and one which is a trigger. For these two say why they helped cause the War

   If the Archduke had not been shot, would a war still have broken out sooner or later?

Why wasn't it 'all over by Christmas'?

As you saw on page 13, anti-German feeling had been common in Britain for some time. The Germans were seen as 'the enemy'. Although there was a big protest against war a week before it broke out, once Germany invaded Belgium on 3 August many ordinary people felt that declaring war on Germany was the right thing to do. This was seen as a heroic war against 'the German aggressor'. Indeed, by 6 August most people had forgotten about the assassination of Archduke Franz Ferdinand which triggered off the conflict.

> **SOURCE 1** From a speech by David Lloyd George, the Chancellor of the Exchequer, in September 1914
>
> 66 *Belgium has been treated brutally . . . Her cornfields have been trampled down. Her villages have been destroyed. Her men have been killed and her women and children too. What had she done?*
> *The Germans think that we cannot beat them. It will not be easy. It will be a terrible war. But in the end we shall march through terror to triumph.* 99

Anti-war feeling evaporated almost overnight. It was replaced by fierce PATRIOTISM. Throughout Britain (and all over Europe) women cheered as husbands and sons went off to fight in Northern France. There was dancing in the streets and the queues outside the army recruitment offices were enormous.

In Germany Kaiser Wilhelm told his soldiers as they set out to fight 'You'll be home before the leaves have fallen from the trees.'

The British government warned that the War might be a terrible one, and the recruitment posters asked men to sign up 'for three years, or as long as the War lasts'. But the popular feeling was 'It will all be over by Christmas.' One soldier remembered his rush to join the army: 'Our one great fear was that the War would be over before we got there.'

What was planned

Germany and Britain had both drawn up their plans for what to do if war started (see Source 2).

SOURCE 2 A map showing what was meant to happen

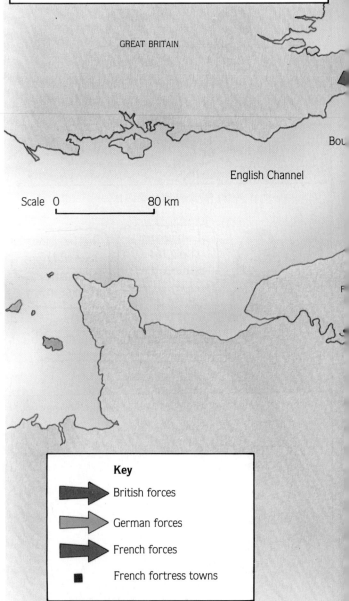

> **Stage 2: the British plan**
> The British plan was to send a small but well trained army (the British Expeditionary Force or BEF) over the Channel to help defend the French and the Belgians.
> Although the Schlieffen Plan was supposed to be a German secret the British expected the Germans to invade through Belgium. If war was declared the BEF would quickly cross to France, take the west flank alongside the French, and halt the German advance.
> The Germans would then be exposed to the east and the west; the Russians, French and British would so greatly outnumber the Germans that they would surrender

GREAT BRITAIN

English Channel

Bou

F

Scale   0   80 km

Key
British forces
German forces
French forces
French fortress towns

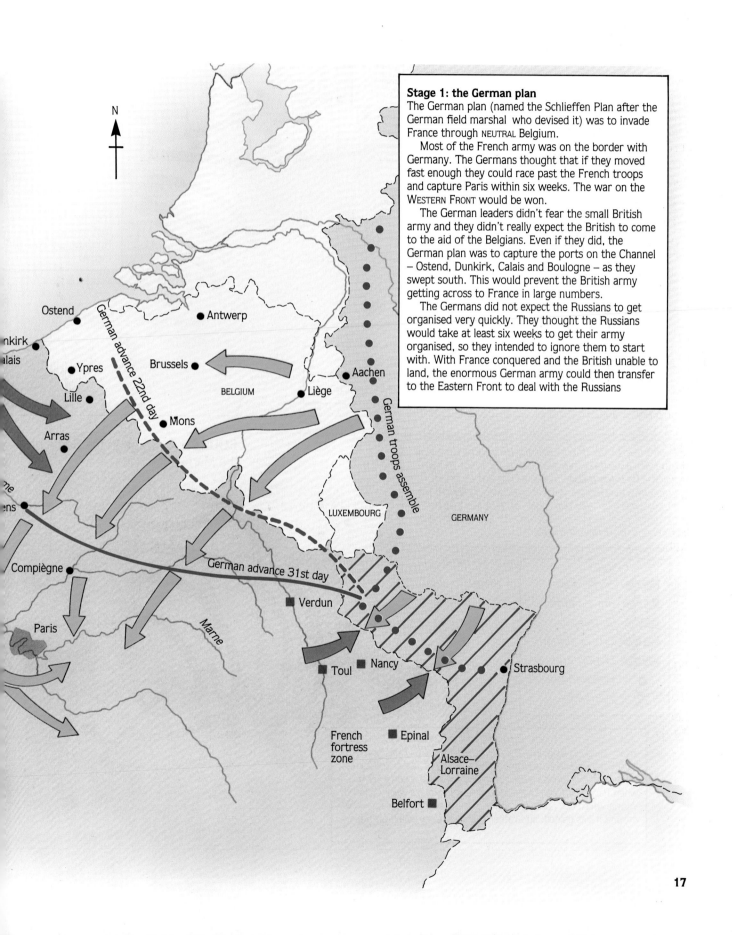

Stage 1: the German plan

The German plan (named the Schlieffen Plan after the German field marshal who devised it) was to invade France through NEUTRAL Belgium.

Most of the French army was on the border with Germany. The Germans thought that if they moved fast enough they could race past the French troops and capture Paris within six weeks. The war on the WESTERN FRONT would be won.

The German leaders didn't fear the small British army and they didn't really expect the British to come to the aid of the Belgians. Even if they did, the German plan was to capture the ports on the Channel – Ostend, Dunkirk, Calais and Boulogne – as they swept south. This would prevent the British army getting across to France in large numbers.

The Germans did not expect the Russians to get organised very quickly. They thought the Russians would take at least six weeks to get their army organised, so they intended to ignore them to start with. With France conquered and the British unable to land, the enormous German army could then transfer to the Eastern Front to deal with the Russians

What actually happened

The Belgians fought so bravely that the German advance was slowed down. Instead of getting to Paris in six weeks, the German army was still fighting in Belgium weeks after it invaded

SOURCE 3 Stage 1: the Germans get stuck in Belgium

The Russians got their army into action much more quickly than the Germans had expected. ten days Russian troops entered Germany. The Germans had to weaken their western armies and transfer troops to the east to prevent the Russians getting any further

As the Germans expected, the French counter-attacked in Alsace and Lorraine. They were well beaten by the Germans

Key
- British forces
- German forces
- French forces
- Fortress towns

Scale 0 — 80 km

The 100,000 men of the British Expeditionary Force were well trained and well equipped. They were ready for action in less than a week – far more quickly than the Germans expected. They fought with the German army at the places shown on the map. The cost was high – by December 1914, more than half of the original BEF were dead – but the western German armies abandoned hope of surrounding Paris

SOURCE 4 Stage 2: the Battle of the Marne

Key
- British attack
- British retreat
- German attack
- German retreat
- French forces
- Fortress towns
- Main battles

Just in time the French responded to the threat of the Germans' attack through Belgium. They switched troops to their border with Belgium and slowed down the advance of the main German army. Reserve troops were rushed out of Paris – some by taxi – when Paris itself was threatened. French soldiers were ordered: 'A unit which can no longer advance must at all costs retain the ground it has gained, and rather than retire, be killed on the spot.'

Scale 0 — 80 km

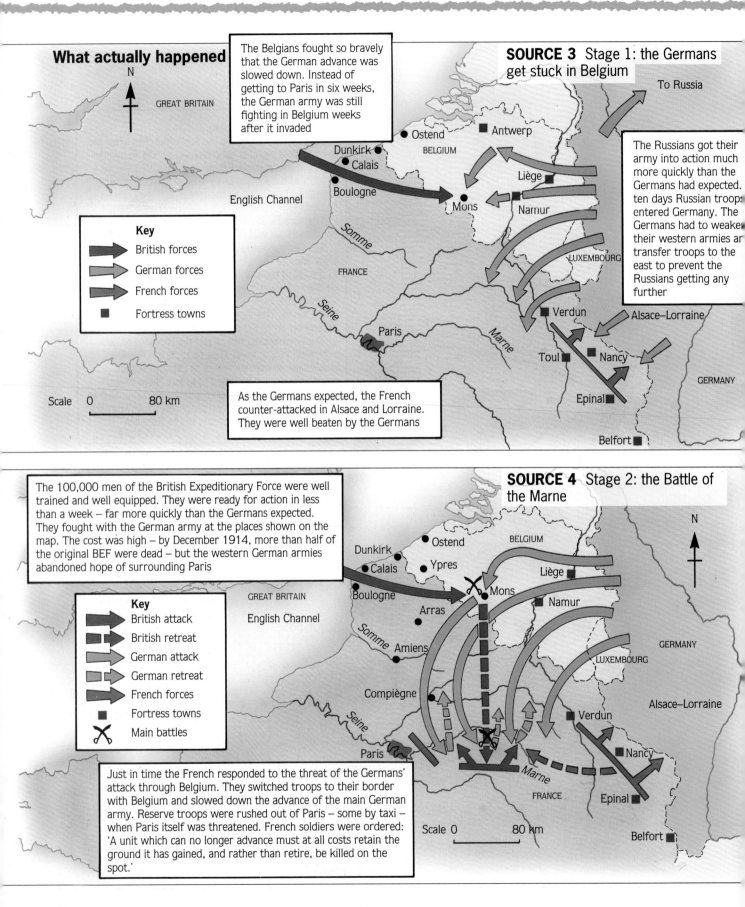

1. List three differences between the plan devised by Schlieffen and what actually happened.
2. Draw a diagram like the one here to show why the Schlieffen Plan failed.

'Why did the Schlieffen Plan fail?'

The war in France and Belgium was planned as 'a war of movement'. The rival armies would manoeuver, trying to outflank or trap their opponents.

By Christmas 1914, however, it was clear that neither side was going to win the quick victory each had predicted to its people. The Schlieffen Plan had failed. Secretly Crown Prince Wilhelm of Germany said, 'We have lost the War. It will go on for a long time but it is already lost.'

Even so, the Germans showed no sign of giving up. And they were strong enough to resist any counter-attack. No one could deliver the knockout blow. The war of movement had been replaced by a STALEMATE. On the Western Front more than two million soldiers were now involved in the War. As the weather got colder and wetter they faced each other over kilometres of increasingly muddy land, churned up by SHELL fire. Both sides began to dig more permanent trenches to protect themselves from enemy machine-gun fire.

By Christmas 1914 a long line of trenches stretched from the English Channel to the Swiss border. These trenches were to be 'home' for the soldiers of both sides for the next three years. Despite millions of casualties, neither army would move more than sixteen kilometres forwards or backwards until well into 1918.

The Germans' only hope was to surround the British and French. They swept round to the north, but the French did the same and neither side was able to trap the other. Meanwhile, the British also headed north to prevent the Germans capturing vital Channel ports such as Calais and Boulogne. They arrived just in time, helped by the Belgians, who delayed the Germans by flooding their land

SOURCE 5 Stage 3: the race for the sea

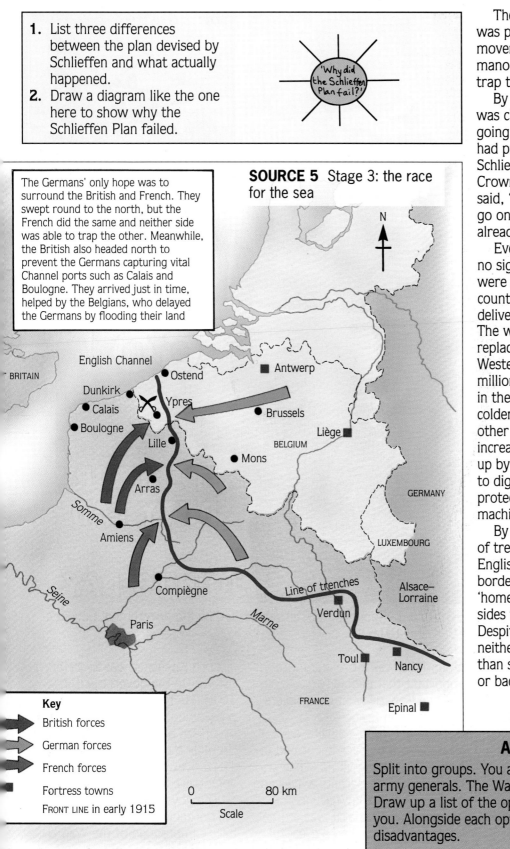

Key

British forces

German forces

French forces

Fortress towns

FRONT LINE in early 1915

0   80 km

Scale

Activity

Split into groups. You are either British or German army generals. The War has reached a stalemate. Draw up a list of the options that are available to you. Alongside each option list its advantages and disadvantages.

The Western Front: the view from Britain

WHEN war broke out the government had most of Britain on its side. Even the Suffragettes and the strikers stopped their protests and helped the war effort. When the government asked for 100,000 volunteer soldiers the response was far better than anyone expected – 750,000 men joined the army in one month.

The public were quickly deluged with PROPAGANDA, including pamphlets, posters, newspaper reports and advertisements. These showed that the War was a just war, that Germany was evil, that Britain would beat Germany, and that soldiers would feel proud to have been part of it.

SOURCE 1 Recruiting posters published by the government between 1914 and 1916

1. Explain as carefully as you can how each poster in Source 1 is trying to persuade men to join up. Are they all using the same methods?
2. Explain why none of these posters show the conditions on the Western Front.
3. Design your own poster to persuade young men to join the army in 1914.

The propaganda deliberately did not show what was actually happening on the Western Front. Neither the new soldiers nor their families knew the horrors of the War that were awaiting them across the Channel. The recruiting posters and government propaganda gave the impression that a soldier's life was heroic, adventurous and rather romantic. In 1914 this was fairly easy as it was still mainly professional soldiers who were doing the fighting, and casualties among the volunteers remained low. As the years went on and casualties mounted it was more and more important that people had a positive view of what the soldiers were doing in France.

More and more soldiers were needed, so the government had to persuade men to join up. They also had to persuade parents, wives and girlfriends that the War was worthwhile and that it was a great adventure rather than a dreadful reality.

Lord Kitchener was Secretary for War in the government in 1914. He had the job of persuading men to sign up. He organised a poster campaign, and 54 million posters were issued. By 1916 over two million men had volunteered.

The government was not the only organisation trying to give a heroic impression of the War, as you can see from Sources 2–5.

SOURCE 2 A poem published in the *Daily Mail* on 12 July 1916. It describes the incident shown in Source 4, which happened on the first day of the Battle of the Somme

> *On through the hail of slaughter*
> *Where gallant comrades fall,*
> *Where blood is poured like water*
> *They drive the trickling ball.*
> *The fear of death before them*
> *Is but an empty name;*
> *True to the land that bore them*
> *The Surreys play the game!*

▼**SOURCE 3** 'Time for one more'
– a cigarette advertisement

TIME FOR ONE MORE

MITCHELL'S GOLDEN DAWN CIGARETTES.

THINKING OF YOU (1).
(A SOLDIER'S LOVE SONG.)

The time seems long and dreary, in foreign lands I roam;
I'm thinking of you, my sweetheart, and of the dear old home.
While sitting here so lonely, there stirs a gentle breeze,
And I seem to hear your voice, dear, 'mid the whisper of the trees.

▲**SOURCE 5** A postcard published for soldiers to send home

▲**SOURCE 4** A picture from the *Illustrated London News* of 29 July 1916 entitled *The Surreys Play the Game*. It shows men from the East Surrey Regiment kicking a football as they launch an attack

4. Look at Sources 1–5. Choose three words from this list to describe the soldiers shown in these sources: cowardly, brave, frightened, heroic, relaxed, stupid, suffering, happy. Explain why you have chosen your three words.
5. You are eighteen years old in 1914. You have spent all your life in a small village, where you have been bored. You want some adventure, you want your parents to be proud of you, and you want to see the world. Use Sources 1–5 to explain why you are joining the army.

The newspapers regularly ran optimistic reports of how the War was going. But there was no way for people to check how accurate these reports were. Letters from soldiers in France were strictly CENSORED. Newspapers themselves were censored from 1915 onwards.

Throughout the War there was a strict rule that no photographs could be published that showed a dead British soldier. Following a major battle casualty lists were sometimes not made public for weeks. And according to the editor of the *Daily Express* the newspapers chose not to focus on casualty stories. He wrote in his diary on 24 October 1914, 'The first eight or ten casualties had as much publicity as the rest put together.'

Activity
Write out a conversation that might take place between a mother and her son who is leaving for the Western Front. The conversation should describe their attitudes and feelings towards the War. Make sure you include what they think the fighting is going to be like.

What was life really like on the Western Front?

MOST people in Britain had a very inaccurate view of what soldiers were going to meet when they crossed the sea to France.

There were over two million men in the British army. Most of them served on the Western Front. Each of these soldiers was a unique individual. His experience of going to war was different from every other soldier's. We are going to use the soldiers' own letters, diaries and poems, as well as official photographs and documents of the time, to try to reconstruct life on the Western Front.

Anyone between the ages of nineteen and 41 could volunteer, although there are plenty of stories of teenagers and older men lying about their age in order to join the army. The soldiers were drawn from all classes of society and from all regions of Britain and its Empire. A large part of Britain's army in the battles in the Middle East was made up of Indian soldiers. Some Indians, as well as Canadians, West Indians, Australians and New Zealanders, also fought on the Western Front in France (see pages 32–33).

Kitting out and training

There were so many volunteers that many of them had to wait weeks or months for equipment. They DRILLED with wooden sticks in place of real rifles.

Some of the training was very hard – ten hours a day of hard physical effort. Some of it was next to useless (see Source 1).

> **SOURCE 1** Written by a soldier, Gerald Brenan
>
> *For three mornings we marched about on the parade ground . . . We were not taught how to fight in trenches. These we were told were only temporary.*

---

1. Look at Sources 2 and 3. How many of the items mentioned in Source 3 can you see on the soldier in Source 2?
2. Using Sources 2 and 3, draw a picture of a soldier and label his equipment.
3. Is there anything in Source 2 that suggests that the photograph was staged?

▶ **SOURCE 2** A photograph of a soldier leaving for France

> **SOURCE 3** List of the kit a British soldier carried with him into the trenches in 1915. The total weight was 30 kilos
>
> *■ Mark II Lee Enfield Rifle*
> *■ large canvas pack for carrying woolly cap, spare socks and greatcoat*
> *■ digging tool – handle and head separate*
> *■ haversack for carrying rations, paybook, toothbrush, soap and towel, spare bootlaces, mess tin [to eat from] and cover, fork and spoon, mending and darning kit*
> *■ full water bottle and carrier*
> *■ bayonet [a blade that could be attached to the end of the rifle]*
> *■ 150 rounds of ammunition in belt and pouches*
> *■ identity tag*
> *■ two canvas bags to carry a respirator and a gas mask*
> *■ service cap and regimental cap badge.*

Arrival in France

Most volunteers were in a Battalion or County Regiment of 1000 men. A Regiment was split up into smaller units of a Company (240 men), a Platoon (60 men) or a Section (fourteen men). Most volunteer soldiers could expect to be serving with men from their own home area, or even with friends from before the War. They often served in 'Pals' Regiments' such as 'The Bradford Lads' or 'The Derby Lads'. These friendships helped support many soldiers through the boredom and the horrors of trench warfare.

They travelled over to France – usually by night – in open topped boats. Early in the War there was little risk of being attacked by German U-boats (submarines). They landed at Channel ports such as Le Havre.

Once in France the soldier would not usually be sent to the front line straight away. He would live in a temporary camp or a COMMANDEERED building for further training and preparation.

> **SOURCE 5** From the autobiography of Gerald Brenan, published in 1968
>
> *In March 1915, we found ourselves in billets in a farmhouse near Armentières on the Belgian frontier. The country around us was green and lush, with more civilians than soldiers. In contrast with this was the continual sound of the guns.*
>
> *A few days later, my company had a short spell in the trenches near Messines . . . As I stood looking at the German lines, the sentry next to me was shot in the head and fell back dead. But I was too excited by the novelty of everything to be affected by this, my first sight of death. I was young and full of life – it could not happen to me.*

1. Do you think it is a good idea that soldiers serve with people from their own home area?
2. Look at Sources 4 and 5. What were Henry Williamson's and Gerald Brenan's reactions to their first sight of war?

> **SOURCE 4** Written in 1973 by the novelist Henry Williamson, who went to France in 1914
>
> *We landed at Le Havre and after one night in a rest camp found ourselves in a series of trucks.*
>
> *At St Omer we marched to a convent, where we practised advances in formation across old stubble, and rumours said we were 'for it'. That night six of us stood among the trees of the garden and watched flickerings in the faraway eastern sky and heard the boom of heavy guns.*
>
> *Next morning we marched north along a straight road between rows of elms and so to Wipers [the British soldiers' name for Ypres]. We slept that night in the cloth hall.*
>
> *In the morning the bugles sounded the alarm . . . Up the Menin Road we marched when coming towards us were prams holding silent children, wounded soldiers, refugees with sacks filled with dead chickens and 40 tall soldiers with staring eyes and hollow cheeks.*
>
> *We were not needed [at the front] and returned to Ypres . . . and marching south found ourselves in a large wood of oaks. There we remained interested and content for the weather was warm. We slept in bunkers made of oak posts and sand bags.*

SOURCE 6 The Worcestershire Regiment going into action – a photograph taken on 28 June 1916

SOURCE 7 The road from Menin to Ypres, the main route to the front-line trenches at Ypres, in 1917

WHAT WAS LIFE REALLY LIKE ON THE WESTERN FRONT?

Up to the front line

The front line was made up of trenches which stretched for hundreds of kilometres, from the coast of Belgium to the border of Switzerland. The soldiers were sent up to the front line for various reasons: in preparation for an attack, to defend against a German attack, or to keep the trenches repaired. Each company was supposed to spend a maximum of six days per month in the front-line trenches, but in practice many soldiers could spend months at a time there – if they survived.

The front-line trenches were backed up by support trenches, communication trenches, dead-end trenches (to confuse the enemy) and large DUGOUTS.

The area between the two sides was known as 'No Man's Land'. Any attack across this area would be slowed down by metres of barbed wire and by the murderous fire from machine-gun posts which could wipe out a whole company in minutes.

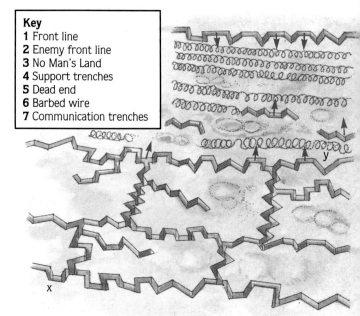

Key
1 Front line
2 Enemy front line
3 No Man's Land
4 Support trenches
5 Dead end
6 Barbed wire
7 Communication trenches

SOURCE 8 The trench system

Activity

The view from the trenches

Draw a large circle on a piece of plain card. This is the lens of a periscope, through which you are looking at the German lines across 'No Man's Land'. Use the evidence to draw inside the circle what you might see through the lens.

1. Copy Source 8 into your book and number the features correctly using the key. Mark German trenches in one colour and British trenches in another colour.
2. Why do you think the trenches were designed in a zig-zag pattern?
3. On your own copy of Source 8 show the route a platoon of soldiers could take to make their way from x to y on the plan.

SOURCE 9 An artist's view of a trench

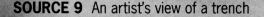

Life in the trenches

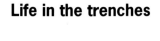

SOURCE 10 From a children's comic of 1992

1. This comic would not claim to be a serious piece of history, but do you think it might be able to give us an accurate picture of life in the trenches? Make a list of things that you think are likely to be accurate/inaccurate in Source 10. Then compare your ideas with the information in Sources 11–19 over the page.

SOURCE 11 A British soldier made this list of daily rations in his notebook

> Bully (corned) beef   1lb. [454g]
> Bread or biscuits   1¼lbs [567g]
> Bacon   ¼lb. [113g]
> Tea   ½oz. [14g]
> Sugar   2oz. [56g]
> Jam   2oz. [56g]
> Cheese   1oz. [28g]
> Butter   ¾oz. [21g]
> Potatoes   ¾lb. [340g]
>
> Also: small amounts of salt, pepper and mustard.

SOURCE 12 Mealtime for the front-line troops at a field kitchen in October 1916

1. Is the soldier in Source 11 well fed?
2. Many soldiers complained about their food, especially once they were sent up to the front-line trenches. Why do you think they complained?

For the soldiers in the trenches the mood varied between discomfort, boredom, anxiety and uncertainty.

The soldiers' life was greatly affected by the weather. In rain their trenches could be knee-deep in water. In winter the mud could freeze as hard as rock. In summer it could bake in blistering heat.

For much of the time shells were falling, so working, sleeping or eating the soldiers had to live with the fear of being killed by an exploding shell.

The front-line trenches were most active at night. An attack was always most likely at night, so sentries had to keep a careful watch, while others repaired defences or barbed wire, or carried out scouting and spying missions.

Despite the constant dangers of trench life, the daytime was mostly very boring. Some soldiers tried to sleep. Others just sat around reading, or smoking, or playing cards. There were also routine jobs to do, such as filling sandbags, cleaning latrines and fetching supplies.

3. Each of the written sources on pages 26–27 describes a problem facing the soldiers. Put a heading in your book which you think best describes the problem, e.g. Source 13 could be 'Water' or 'Animals'. Underneath each heading, explain what the problem was, and how it affected the soldiers.

SOURCE 13 A journalist's view of trenches during the Battle of the Somme

> The water in the trenches through which we waded was alive with a multitude of swimming frogs. Red slugs crawled up the side of the trenches and strange beetles with dangerous looking horns wriggled along dry ledges and invaded the dugouts, in search of the lice which infested them.

SOURCE 14 By Sergeant Harry Roberts, who lived in a flooded trench for six days

> If you have never had trench feet described to you, I will explain. Your feet swell to two or three times their normal size and go completely dead. You could stick a bayonet into them and not feel a thing.
>
> If you are lucky enough not to lose your feet and the swelling begins to go down, it is then that the indescribable agony begins. I have heard men cry and scream with the pain and many have had to have their feet and legs amputated.
>
> I was one of the lucky ones, but one more day in that trench and it may have been too late.

SOURCE 15 The last letter from Private Peter MacGregor to his wife in September 1916. He was killed shortly afterwards by a direct hit on his trench by an enemy shell

> *I am well and looking forward to the end of the War. I wish it would hurry up.*
>
> *One of our men was caught by a sniper – he was standing at the entrance to his dugout, the bullet went in under his shoulder – alas, alas.*
>
> *When I was standing at the cookhouse door, I saw the stretcher which came along to take the poor fellow away – how sad it was, he was carried out, wrapped up in his waterproof sheet, placed in this thing and whisked away.*
>
> *The business of the hour has to go on. A dead man is no use to the army, get him out of the way as quickly as possible. War is a terrible thing and so few people realise it.*

SOURCE 16 From *Goodbye to All That*, the novelist Robert Graves' account of his experiences during the War

> *To get a 'cushy' one [an injury bad enough to get you sent home] is all the old hands think about.*
>
> *Bloke in the Camerons wanted a 'cushy', bad! Fed up and far from home he was. He puts his hand over the top and gets a trigger finger taken off, and two more besides. 'I'm off to bonny Scotland!' he says, laughing. But on the way down the trench to the dressing station [where wounds were treated], he forgets to stoop low where the old sniper's working. He gets it through the head.*

SOURCE 17 An official account of a court martial (a military trial) in 1916. This soldier had been one of the first to enlist in 1914

> *No 1 . . . 2 Private A . . . B . . . the Battalion (Pioneers) South Staffordshire Regiment was tried by FGCM on the following charge: 'Misbehaving in such a manner as to show cowardice.' The accused, when proceeding with a party for work in the trenches, ran away owing to the bursting of a shell and did not afterwards rejoin the party.*
>
> *The sentence of the court was 'to suffer death by being shot'. The sentence was duly carried out at 5.50 a.m. on 18 October 1916.*

SOURCE 18 From an interview with driver R.L. Venables

> *Whilst asleep during the night, we were frequently awakened by rats running over us. When this happened too often for my liking, I would lie on my back and wait for a rat to linger on my legs; then violently heave my legs upward, throwing the rat into the air. Occasionally, I would hear a grunt when the rat landed on a fellow victim.*

SOURCE 19 A British trench photographed in 1916

The soldiers faced all these problems before they had even seen a German. The worst was yet to come.

4. The soldiers in Sources 16 and 17 tried to get away from the fighting. Which one do you have most sympathy with and why?
5. Why do you think the soldier in Source 17 was executed?
6. Now that you have studied these sources about life in the trenches, how accurate do you think Source 10 is?
7. Do you think the fact that the artist of Source 10 was drawing for a children's comic influenced the kind of pictures he drew?

Preparations for attack

There was no way of getting round the ends of your enemy's trenches, so the only means of attacking the enemy was through a full-frontal attack – charging at the enemy trenches. The generals were convinced that if they could only get enough soldiers 'over the top', charging in a human wave, then they would break through the enemy defences and capture their trenches. Throughout 1915, full-frontal attacks were launched to try to break the deadlock. Battles at Neuve Chapelle, Compiègne, Ypres, Arras and Loos resulted in the British and the ALLIES losing nearly 400,000 dead for a gain in territory of about ten square kilometres. This was trench warfare!

Whenever a major attack was planned, there was ground or aircraft RECONNAISSANCE to check out the enemy position. The soldiers were informed well beforehand. Before the attack there were massive ARTILLERY BOMBARDMENTS, which were aimed to weaken the enemy defences but which would also warn the enemy that an attack was on its way.

When the whistle sounded, often at dawn, the soldiers began the advance across 'No Man's Land' towards the German lines. They knew the chances of survival were slim, and they realised that many of these attacks were totally pointless and rarely gained anything worthwhile, but orders had to be obeyed.

SOURCE 20 From A.P. Herbert's war novel *The Secret Battle*, published in 1919. The author served as a soldier on the Western Front. In this extract plans are being laid for an attack on the enemy trenches

66 *There was a theory that this particular section of enemy trench had been evacuated . . . Harry was told to get right up to that trench, to look in, and see what was in it. It was a thing he had done twice before . . . It meant the usual breathless, toilsome wriggle across No Man's Land, avoiding the flares and the two snipers who covered that bit of the ground, finding a gap in the wires, getting through without being seen, without noise, without catching his clothes on a wandering barb, or banging his revolver against a multitude of tin cans. Then you had to listen and wait and if possible look in the trench.*

When (and if) you had done that you had to get back . . . past the same obstacles, the same snipers.

However, Harry was a scout and it was his job. 99

SOURCE 21 From *Goodbye to All That*, by the novelist Robert Graves

66 *On 19 September 1915, we relieved the Middlesex Regiment at Cambrin and were told that these would be the trenches from which we attacked.*

The bombardment had already started a week in advance . . . The trenches shook and a great cloud of drifting shell-smoke hid the German lines. Shells went over our heads in a steady stream; we had to shout to make our neighbours hear.

Dying down a little at night, the racket began every morning at dawn . . . More casualties came from our 'shorts' and 'blow-backs' [British shells which landed close to British trenches] than from German shells. I got two small wounds on the hand. 99

SOURCE 22 Written by a photographer, Geoffrey Malins, who was sent to France by the government to photograph the Battle of the Somme. He is describing the night before the start of the Battle of the Somme

66 *Crowds of men were crouching round, heating up their canteens of water, some frying pieces of meat, others heating soup, and all the time laughing and talking. From other groups came the quiet humming of favourite songs . . . And these men knew they were going over the top in the morning. They knew that many would not be alive tomorrow night, yet I never saw a sad face, nor heard a word of complaint . . .* 99

Over the top

SOURCE 23 These are stills from an official British film made in 1916. Some historians think this was a staged event

SOURCE 24 Crawling to the German trenches under fire – this photograph was taken on a training exercise

SOURCE 25 Written by Private Henry Russell about the Battle of the Somme in 1916

During our advance, I saw many of my colleagues killed by German machine gun fire, but this somehow or other did not seem to worry me and I continued to go forward until I suddenly became aware that there were few of us left capable of going on.

I found myself in the company of an officer, Lieutenant Wallace. We dived into a flat, shallow hole made by our guns, not knowing what to do next . . . I came to the conclusion that going on would be suicidal and that the best thing we could do would be to stay there and try to pick off any Germans who might expose themselves. Lieut. Wallace said, however, that we had been ordered to go on at all costs and that we must comply with this order. At this, he stood up and within a few seconds dropped down riddled with bullets. This left me with the same problem and having observed his action, I felt that I must do the same. I stood up and was immediately hit by two bullets and dropped down . . .

I am now convinced that when it comes to the crunch, nobody has any fear at all.

Activity

Write a diary for a period of one week in November 1915, starting on a Monday. Your diary could include information from any of the sources in this section or from previous sections. It should include details about trench conditions and an attack when you went 'over the top'.

The aftermath

During the War almost a million soldiers of the British Empire were killed. Germany and Russia each lost nearly two million dead, France and Austria–Hungary each lost a million and a half and Italy half a million. It was the machine guns on both sides that accounted for most of the dead. It may seem suicidal to have kept on sending troops across 'No Man's Land', but throughout the years 1914 to 1917 those were the tactics used by the generals from HQ (headquarters), far behind the front lines. Little was gained during this time.

SOURCE 26 Casualties of the Battle of the Somme

But orders had to be obeyed and it was only very rarely that soldiers refused. There was a serious mutiny in the French army in April 1917 which led to 55 soldiers being executed. In September 1917 there was a riot by several thousand British and Commonwealth soldiers at the Army Base Camp in Etaples, but most historians see this as a protest against conditions rather than an anti-war protest. In the whole War 332 British soldiers were executed for offences such as cowardice (see Source 17 on page 27).

---

1. Sources 20–26 include extracts from novels, eye-witness reports, staged photographs and real life photographs. Make a list of the problems involved in using each type of evidence to understand what it was like to be involved in an attack on the German trenches.

Behind the lines

Wounded soldiers often depended on the bravery of their mates, who would have to carry them back to their own trenches. Many of the wounded died in 'No Man's Land' because there was no one to help them. But the lucky ones would be carried back to makeshift hospitals and DRESSING STATIONS behind the lines – beyond the reach of the machine guns and shells.

There were many soldiers and support workers working behind the lines. This was where the War was run. This was where thousands of casualties were cared for. This was where supplies of weapons, food, medicines and clothes were stored and organised for the whole British Army. This was where most of the women who had enlisted in the Voluntary Aid Detachments (VAD) – a nursing group – and the First Aid Nursing Auxiliary (FANY) were working.

SOURCE 27 Victims of poison gas at a dressing station

SOURCE 28 Mairi Chisholm and Elizabeth, Baroness de T'Serclaes driving an ambulance through the ruins of the French town of Pervyse in 1917. Both had joined FANY

Some men saw a job behind the lines as a 'cushy' (easy) option. As the War progressed and more manpower was needed in the fighting lines, womanpower became more and more important in the support services behind the lines. In 1917 12,000 men were working behind the lines in France. The generals decided that women should do most of these jobs: cooking, cleaning, typing letters and official documents, and medical duties. So in 1917 the Women's Army Auxiliary Corps (WAAC) was set up as a separate army unit, serving in difficult and dangerous conditions. The women had no special privileges and suffered the same hardships as the men they replaced.

> **SOURCE 29** From Elizabeth de T'Serclaes' autobiography
>
> 66 *We slept in our clothes and cut our hair short so that it would tuck inside our caps. Dressing meant simply putting on our boots . . . There were times when we had to scrape the lice off with the blunt edge of a knife and our underclothes stuck to us.* 99

> **SOURCE 30** From a book about women in the War by a modern historian, Roy Terry
>
> 66 *On 30 May 1918, eight women were killed in a raid on Camp 1 at Abbeville in Northern France. Seven others were wounded, one of whom died later. The bravery of the survivors earned commendations from all and three military medals were awarded to the women who helped in the rescue . . .*
>
> *Up to this time, the only women killed had been hospital personnel, and newspaper reporters were keen to have a go at the enemy for killing women . . . However, it was pointed out that because the women were replacing combatants, the enemy could be excused for killing them if he could.* 99

1. Make a list of all the types of work that women did in support of the front-line troops.
2. What was the main reason for the setting up of the WAAC?
3. What does this tell you about attitudes towards women at the time?
4. How important do you think women's support role was?

Back home again

Some wounded soldiers recovered behind the lines. Others were sent back to Britain. There were those with shell-shock – a kind of nervous breakdown brought on by the War. There were those who'd been blinded or had their lungs corroded by a poison gas attack. There were those who had lost legs, feet or hands, or been badly burned. Boats regularly crossed the Channel taking the sick and even the dying back to Britain.

Healthy soldiers went home too, on LEAVE. Some soldiers went home on official duties.

Each of them carried with him his own memories of the experiences of War. Now they faced a new problem – what to say to their family and friends about the horrors of the War on the Western Front.

Who fought for the British on the Western Front?

WHEN the War began, the British Army was small compared with those of other countries. As we have seen, there were huge numbers of volunteers from Britain. This took the overall number in the British Army to near two million. These included regiments from Scotland, Wales and Ireland as well as England.

But more men were needed. Britain called upon different parts of the Empire for support. The so-called 'Empire armies' (under British command) played a crucial role on the Western Front.

The drawings on these pages were made by a British soldier, A.D. Langhorne, who was serving on the Western Front. They show some of the people who were fighting for the British in France.

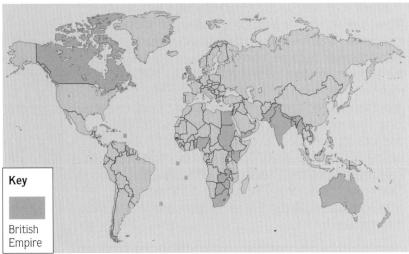

Key

British Empire

From Australia:

The Australian Imperial Force (AIF) reached France in March 1916, having already been involved in the Gallipoli campaign in Turkey (see pages 66–71). They were a wholly volunteer army.

Over 300,000 Australians fought on all war fronts, the majority in France where 175,000 were killed or wounded. They fought in many battles including the Somme, Ypres and Passchendaele.

From India:

The picture shows a Bengal lancer in an Indian CAVALRY division. Indian soldiers and cavalry, including Sikhs and Gurkhas, were in action on the Western Front as early as October 1914. They played a key role in the British sectors of the front during early German attacks when the British were very stretched.

On 31 October 1914 Sepoy Khudadad of the 129th Baluchis won the Victoria Cross for keeping his machine gun firing when all his comrades had been killed by the Germans. But when his machine-gun post was eventually overrun by the enemy, he was bayoneted and left for dead.

Over 138,000 Indian troops fought, and 5000 were killed in France. Many were withdrawn during 1915 to fight on other fronts, particularly Egypt and Mesopotamia (see Sources 2 and 3 on pages 73–74). Around a million Indian soldiers fought on all fronts.

From Canada:

Canada was one of the first countries to respond to the call for forces. Canadian troops arrived in the trenches in April 1915. Probably their most famous success was the capture of Vimy Ridge, a great prize. Around 400,000 Canadians fought on the Western Front (60,000 killed).

When the Germans launched their last main offensive in March 1918, they avoided the part of the front where the Canadians were: many Canadians considered this was an acknowledgement of their reputation as tough fighters.

From New Zealand:

One of the most highly regarded fighting units on the Western Front was the New Zealand Division. Around 100,000 fighting men came to France, of whom 13,500 did not return home and 35,000 were wounded.

Sergeant Dick Travis was awarded the Victoria Cross for extreme bravery. He captured two machine guns and killed their crews in a night operation. When an enemy officer and three men rushed to retake the guns, he killed them single-handed. He was killed 24 hours later.

From the Carribean:

Eleven battalions of West Indian INFANTRY, over 15,000 men, were recruited from various islands including Jamaica, Trinidad, Grenada and Barbados. They wanted to fight as soldiers. However, when they reached France, they found that they were to be used to unload ships, and supply troops at the front with ammunition. How far this was due to racism is difficult to tell, but they resented the fact that they were not able to fight. They were badly housed and found it difficult to adjust to the cold conditions. Over 1000 died of sickness and 185 were killed by the enemy.

Later, two battalions did see action in Palestine where they fought in the Jordan Valley. They were highly praised for their bravery.

Discussion

Some books on the First World War do not mention the wide range of nationalities who fought on the Western Front. Why do you think this is? Why do you think it matters?

Coming home

FOR the British soldier returning from the trenches on leave, Britain was a longed-for haven. Yet many of them did not actually enjoy their time back in 'Blighty'. The terrible experiences they had been through set them apart from people in Britain. One CIVILIAN described the returning soldiers as 'like strange beings from another world . . . stained with the mud of the trenches.' To the soldier Britain also seemed strange, with everybody so enthusiastic about the War. You can read what one soldier felt in Source 1.

> **SOURCE 1** A description of the thoughts of a wounded soldier back in England by the historian R.H. Tawney, who was wounded during the Battle of the Somme
>
> 66 *The Tommy [soldier] we read about in the magazines is a creature at once ridiculous and disgusting. He is shown as 'cheerful' and enjoying the 'excitement' of war, of finding 'sport' in killing other men, or hunting Germans out of dugouts as a terrier hunts rats.*
>
> *Of the soldier's internal life, the sensation of taking part in a game played by monkeys and organised by lunatics, you realise, I think, nothing.* 99

The cartoons on this page bring together the experiences of four different soldiers.

1. Try to explain why each soldier in the cartoons finds it difficult to make people understand what the War is really like.
2. Have you any advice for each of the soldiers?

35

Images and impressions of war

MEN from all walks of life joined the army, and among them were many artists. There was even a regiment called 'The Artists' Rifles'. The government realised how valuable these artists could be to its propaganda campaign. The Ministry of Information – which was in charge of propaganda – thought war artists would be particularly useful in convincing neutral countries, such as the USA, either to stay neutral or, better still, to join the War on the Allies' side. They therefore employed official war artists to record scenes from the War. The main restriction on the artists was that no picture could be displayed which showed a dead British soldier.

Pictures by official war artists, such as those in Sources 1–5, were used to illustrate books and pamphlets put out by the government. They were also shown in exhibitions all around the country.

1. If you were trying to convince the USA to join the War on the Allies' side what kind of pictures would you want to be able to show them?

▶ SOURCE 1 *The Menin Road* by Paul Nash (1889–1946). He joined up in 1914, and served at Ypres in 1916. While wounded in 1917 he painted more than 60 paintings in eight weeks for an exhibition in London. The government was so impressed with his pictures that they made him an official war artist in November 1917. This picture shows the road out of Ypres

▶ SOURCE 2 *Over the Top* by John Nash (1893–1977).He was Paul Nash's younger brother. He joined the army in September 1916. He served in France from November 1916 to January 1918, when he was made an official war artist

▲SOURCE 3 *Paths of Glory* by C.R.W. Nevinson (1889–1946). He joined the Red Cross in 1914, working as a driver, interpreter and stretcher-bearer in France, and with the Army Medical Corps at a hospital in London. His own health was ruined by the War and he was invalided out in January 1916. He exhibited some of his war paintings in London in September 1916, and was made a war artist in 1917. He was sent to France for the early weeks of the Battle of Passchendaele. This picture was painted in 1917, but not exhibited until after the War because of the ban on showing dead British soldiers

SOURCE 4 *The Machine Gunners* by C.R.W. Nevinson (see Source 3)

SOURCE 5 *Gassed* by John Singer Sargent (1856–1925) He was aged 60 when the government sent him to France in 1918 to paint a picture to symbolise the co-operation of the British and the Americans. He quickly abandoned his official project, and painted instead the scenes he saw behind the lines – including this clearing station for casualties of a mustard gas attack

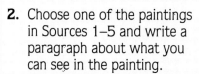

2. Choose one of the paintings in Sources 1–5 and write a paragraph about what you can see in the painting.
3. Elsewhere in this book there are photographs showing similar places and events to those in Sources 1–5. Look up Source 1 on page 48, Source 23 on page 29, Source 27 on page 30, Source 7 on page 23 and Source 26 on page 30 and match them to Sources 1–5.
4. Compare the painting you wrote about for question 2 with the photograph of the same subject. Does it give the same impression or a different impression of that aspect of the War?
5. All the painters and photographers experienced the War at first hand. Which type of evidence – photos or paintings – would you consider to be:
a) the most reliable record of the War
b) the most useful for showing what the War was really like?
6. Why do you think the government wanted painters to record the War as well as photographers?

Activity
You have been invited to select photos and paintings for an exhibition on the First World War. You can choose paintings or photos from anywhere in this book.
1. Which three will you choose to show how terrible the War was?
2. Which three will you choose to show how heroic the War was?

37

Poetry

Thousands of words of poetry were written during the First World War. You have already seen one example (Source 2 on page 21). Some of the poetry was sentimental nonsense, but the best of it managed to put into words the compassion, the anger, the frustration, the glory and the stupidity of war, in a way that prose could not. See what you think.

SOURCE 6 *A Working Party* by Siegfried Sassoon (1886–1967). He served in the army for most of the War, and became increasingly angry about the way the generals were running it. This poem was written in 1917

*. . . Three hours ago he stumbled up the trench
Now he will never walk that road again:
He must be carried back, a jolting lump
Beyond all need of tenderness and care.*

*He was a young man with a meagre wife
And two small children in a Midland town;
He showed their photographs to all his mates,
And they considered him a decent chap
Who did his work and hadn't much to say,
And always laughed at other people's jokes
Because he hadn't any of his own.*

*That night when he was busy at his job
Of piling bags along the parapet,
He thought how slow time went, stamping his feet
And blowing on his fingers, pinched with cold.
He thought of getting back by half-past twelve,
And tot of rum to send him warm to sleep
In draughty dugout frowsty with the fumes
Of coke, and full of snoring, weary men.*

*He pushed another bag along the top,
Craning his body outward; then a flare
Gave one glimpse of No Man's Land and wire,
And as he dropped his head the instant split
His startled life with lead, and all went out.*

SOURCE 7 *To My Brother (In Memory of July 1st 1916)* by Vera Brittain (1893–1970). Her brother, Captain Edward Brittain, won a Military Cross medal at the Battle of the Somme in 1916 and died on 15 June 1918, four days after the poem was written

*Your battle-wounds are scars upon my heart,
Received when in that grand and tragic 'show'
        You played your part
        Two years ago,*

*And silver in the summer morning sun
I see the symbol of your courage glow —
        That Cross you won
        Two years ago.*

*Though now again you watch the shrapnel fly,
And hear the guns that daily louder grow,
        As in July
        Two years ago,*

*May you endure to lead the Last Advance,
And with your men pursue the flying foe,
        As once in France
        Two years ago.*

SOURCE 8 From *The Song of the Mud* by Mary Borden (1887–1968), who ran a mobile hospital at the Western Front. This poem was written in 1917

*This is the hymn of mud – the obscene, the filthy, the putrid,
The vast liquid grave of our armies.
It has drowned our men.
Its monstrous distended belly reeks with the undigested dead.
Our men have gone into it, sinking slowly
        And struggling and slowly disappearing
Our fine men, our brave, strong, young men;*

1. Source 7 could be summed up as 'A woman hopes her brave brother survives the War'; Source 6 could be summed up as 'A dull, ordinary bloke gets shot as a result of his own stupidity'. How have the poets turned their poems into more than this?

2. In Sources 9 and 11 lines have been missed out. Copy out the poems and complete them by adding lines that you think fit well.
3. Compare ideas with other people in the class. Your teacher will tell you what the poets actually wrote.

SOURCE 9 *Trench Idyll* by Richard Aldington (1892–1962). This poem was written in 1918, after he was invalided out of the army

66 *We sat together in the trench,*
He on a lump of frozen earth
Blown in the night before,
I on an unexploded shell;
And smoked and talked, like exiles,
Of ....
How at that very hour
The taxi-cabs were taking folk to dine . . .
Then we sat silent for a while
As a machine gun swept the parapet.

He said:
'I've been here on and off two years
And only seen one man killed.'

'That's odd.'

'The bullet hit him in the throat; He fell in a heap
on the fire-step,
And called out, "My God! DEAD!" '

'Good Lord, how terrible!'

'Well, as to that, the nastiest job I've had
Was last year on this very front
Taking the [identity] discs at night from men
Who'd hung for six months on the wire
Just over there.
The worst of all was

...
Thank God we couldn't see their faces;
They had gas helmets on . . .'

I shivered;
'It's rather cold here, sir, suppose we move?' 99

SOURCE 10 From *1914 – The Soldier* by Rupert Brooke (1887–1915). He died in Greece on his way to fight in Turkey

66 *If I should die, think only this of me:*
That there's some corner of a foreign field
That is forever England. There shall be
In that rich earth a richer dust concealed;
A dust whom England bore, shaped, made aware,
Gave, once, her flowers to love, her ways to roam,
A body of England's, breathing English air,
Washed by the rivers, blest by suns of home . . . 99

SOURCE 11 *In Flanders Fields* by John McCrae (1872–1918). He wrote this poem in 1915 when he was a medical officer in France

66 *In Flanders fields the poppies blow*
Between the crosses, row on row,
That mark our place; and in the sky
The larks, still bravely singing, fly
Scarce heard amid the guns below.

We are the Dead. Short days ago
We lived, felt dawn, saw sunset glow,
Loved and were loved, and now we lie
In Flanders fields.

Take up our quarrel with the foe:
To you from falling hands we throw
The torch; be yours to hold it high.
If ....
We will not sleep, though poppies grow
In Flanders fields. 99

SOURCE 12 From *Dulce et Decorum Est*, written in 1917 by Wilfred Owen (1893–1918). He was killed while serving on the Western Front

66 *If in some smothering dreams you too could pace*
Behind the wagon that we flung him in, . . .
If you could hear, at every jolt, the blood
Come gargling from the froth-corrupted lungs,
Obscene as cancer, bitter as the cud
Of vile, incurable sores on innocent tongues, —
My friend, you would not tell with such high zest
To children ardent for some desperate glory,
The old Lie: Dulce et decorum est Pro patria mori.
[It is sweet and proper to die for your country] 99

4. Do Sources 10 and 12 suggest that it is brave or stupid to die for your country? How?

Activity
Work in pairs. Choose one of the following tasks.
A. Supporters of the War have asked you to produce a poster headlined: 'Fight For Your Country'.
B. Protesters against the War have asked you to produce a poster headlined 'End the Killing'.

Choose a painting from Sources 1–5 and a phrase from Sources 6–12 to use for the poster.

Field Marshal Haig: 'the Butcher of the Somme'?

In December 1915 it was still stalemate on the Western Front. Neither side had made any real progress towards victory, although hundreds of attacks had been launched by either side and hundreds of thousands of soldiers killed.

The British began to question how well their army was being led, and on 10 December 1915 a new commander of the British forces was appointed. He was Field Marshal Haig. He was 54 and he had already had a long and successful military career. In particular he had been a celebrated cavalry commander in the Boer War fifteen years earlier. In that war the British fought against a poorly equipped enemy on the dry plains of South Africa.

Haig faced a difficult task. Trench warfare was a new kind of fighting. Some people had predicted years before the First World War that a European war would end in stalemate with each side dug into trenches. But no one really knew how to cope with trench warfare now it was here. No one knew how to win a war like this. So the generals fell back on the ideas they had used successfully in past wars.

1. Look at Source 1. Do you agree with any of Haig's ideas about warfare?
2. Do you think people at the time would have agreed or disagreed with him?
3. How do you think a) soldiers in France and b) civilians in Britain would react to the news that Haig had been appointed as the new commander?

1907 Success in battle depends mainly on morale and determination.

1915 The way to capture machine guns is by grit and determination.

1916 The machine gun is a much overrated weapon.

1916 We must wear the enemy down as much as possible.

SOURCE 1 Some of Field Marshal Haig's statements about how wars should be fought

SOURCE 2 The Western Front in February 1916

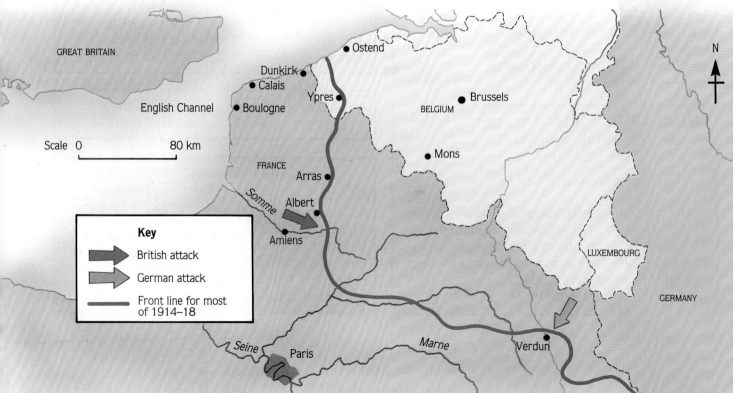

GREAT BRITAIN

English Channel

Ostend
Dunkirk
Calais
Ypres
Boulogne

Brussels
BELGIUM

Scale 0 — 80 km

FRANCE

Mons

Arras

Somme
Albert

Amiens

LUXEMBOURG

GERMANY

Key

→ British attack

→ German attack

— Front line for most of 1914–18

Seine
Paris

Marne

Verdun

In February 1916 the Germans began yet another attack. They sent wave upon wave of soldiers over the top to attack the French forts around the town of Verdun (see Source 2). They did not expect to break through, but they did hope to wear down the morale and strength of the French soldiers. Five months and 700,000 deaths later, the French were still hanging on, but only just. The British desperately needed to relieve the pressure on the French.

So the British High Command led by Field Marshal Haig decided to begin a major attack along the line of the River Somme. They hoped this would draw German soldiers away from the attack on Verdun. Haig also hoped that a British success at the Somme would strengthen the morale of French soldiers. What's more, he had information that suggested that the Germans were outnumbered and that their morale was low.

For a week at the end of June the artillery bombardment took place and then, finally, on 1 July 1916, the order to go over the top was given. Nearly five months later the pressure on Verdun had been lifted, but at the Somme only a few square kilometres of blood and mud had been gained, and hundreds of thousands of soldiers had died. On 18 November 1916, when blizzards covered the area in snow, Field Marshall Haig called a halt to the attack.

This was one of the bloodiest battles in the War. It resulted in more British dead than any battle before it. It has earned Haig the title 'the Butcher of the Somme': the man responsible for unnecessarily, almost casually, sending thousands of young British men to their deaths – for almost no gain at all.

Source 3 gives one example of attitudes to Haig. It comes from a recent BBC television series called *Blackadder Goes Forth*. For six episodes Captain Blackadder and Private Baldrick try to avoid going over the top. Their fellow soldier Lieutenant George is much more enthusiastic. The conversation takes place 'in 1916'.

---

4. Look at Source 3. What impression of Field Marshal Haig does Blackadder give?

My instincts lead me to believe that we are at last about to go over the top.

Great Scott, Sir! You mean the moment has finally arrived for us to give Harry Hun a darn good British style thrashing, six of the best, trousers down?

You mean 'Are we all going to get killed?' Yes. Clearly Field Marshal Haig is about to make yet another giant effort to move his drinks cabinet six inches closer to Berlin.

SOURCE 3 A still from *Blackadder Goes Forth*, showing Lieutenant George on the left and Captain Blackadder on the right

FIELD MARSHAL HAIG: 'THE BUTCHER OF THE SOMME'?

On pages 42–45 we are going to consider whether Haig deserves his bad reputation. We investigate whether he was a bad commander who made mistakes or whether he was simply too ready to accept high casualties. We also consider whether he was out of touch with what was happening at the front line or whether there were simply no alternatives to the tactics he followed.

Using the evidence on these pages, you can compare Haig's statements about the Battle of the Somme with some observations by people who were at the front line.

Haig's views

SOURCE 4 Written by Haig in June 1916 before the battle began

The nation must be taught to bear losses. No amount of skill on the part of the higher commanders, no training, however good, on the part of the officers and men, no superiority of arms and ammunition, however great, will enable victories to be won without the sacrifice of men's lives. The nation must be prepared to see heavy casualty lists.

SOURCE 5 Written by Haig on 30 June 1916, the day before the attack started

The men are in splendid spirits. Several have said that they have never before been so instructed and informed of the nature of the operation before them. The barbed wire has never been so well cut, nor the artillery preparation so thorough. All the commanders are full of confidence.

SOURCE 6 From a report by Haig on the first day of the attack, 1 July 1916

Very successful attack this morning . . . All went like clockwork . . . The battle is going very well for us and already the Germans are surrendering freely. The enemy is so short of men that he is collecting them from all parts of the line. Our troops are in wonderful spirits and full of confidence.

The soldiers' views

- The wire had not been cut.
- The Germans had dug trenches so deep that the bombardment had not caused much damage.
- As a general, Haig never personally visited the front line.

SOURCE 7 From an interview with Private George Coppard, who survived the Battle of the Somme

Hundreds of dead were strung out [on the barbed wire] like wreckage washed up to a high water mark. Quite as many died on the enemy wire as on the ground . . . It was clear that there were no gaps in the wire at the time of attack. The Germans must have been reinforcing the wire for months. It was so thick that daylight could barely be seen through it . . . How did the planners imagine that Tommies [British soldiers] would get through the wire? Who told them that artillery fire would pound such wire to pieces? Any Tommy could have told them that shell fire lifts wire up and drops it down, often in a worse tangle than before.

- There were 60,000 British casualties on the first day of the battle.
- Many German prisoners were taken.
- One Canadian battalion lost 700 out of 850 men!

SOURCE 8 Written in 1988 in a biography of Haig by Gerard De Groot

While Haig slept in a cosy bed in a quiet country chateau and dined on the best food available, his men lived in muddy, noisy trenches sharing their bully beef and biscuits with big, bloated rats. It apparently did not bother Haig that his war was so much more comfortable than that of the men he commanded.

1. Look at Sources 4 and 5. What do you think Haig expected to happen on the first day of the fighting?
2. Why did this not happen?

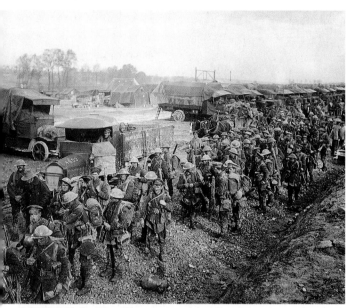

SOURCE 9 The Worcestershire Regiment coming out of the trenches in September 1916, after a three-month stint during the Battle of the Somme

> **3.** Which of the following statements can be supported by Sources 4–8?
> ■ 'Haig was ignorant of what was going on at the front line.'
> ■ 'Haig did not care about the loss of life.'
> ■ 'Haig genuinely believed that the attack was going well.'
> Explain your answer.
> **4.** Compare Source 9 with Source 6 on page 23. Write three sentences commenting on the differences between them.
> **5.** From the evidence so far how do you think Haig expected to win the War?

The view from Britain

The courage and bravery of the troops was never in question. Back in Britain stories of individual heroism were spread with great enthusiasm (see Source 10).

Neville's Attack became a celebrated incident and a picture of it was drawn for a London newspaper in 1916 (see Source 4 on page 21). The Germans, however, used this same picture for very different purposes and circulated it with the following caption in ten different languages: 'An English absurdity: football played during storm attack.'

SOURCE 10 From a letter written by a friend of Captain Wilfred Neville of the East Surrey Regiment to Neville's sister, describing his death at the Battle of the Somme

❝ *Five minutes before zero time, your brother [Wilfred Neville] strolled up in his usual calm way and we shared a last joke before going over.*

The company went over the top very well, with Soames and your brother kicking off with the company footballs. [While on leave, Neville had bought two footballs for his company to kick across No Man's Land at zero hour!] We had to face very heavy rifle and machine gun fire and nearing the front German trench, the line slackened pace slightly. Seeing this, Wilfred dashed in front with a bomb in his hand and was immediately shot through the head . . . ❞

But alongside all the stories of heroism, people in Britain were also receiving daily news of the casualties at the Somme. People were no longer shocked by vast casualty numbers – 20,000 dead were impossible to imagine. But eye-witness reports filtered back to Britain, sometimes in letters such as Source 11 which escaped the army censors. Families came face to face with the horrors of war, maybe for the first time – and face to face with the anger of some of the soldiers having to fight this war.

SOURCE 11 Written by Lieutenant J.A. Raws of the 23rd Battalion in a letter to his family shortly before his death on 23 August 1916

❝ *We are lousy, stinking, ragged, unshaven and sleepless. My tunic is rotten with other men's blood and partly spattered with a friend's brains. It is horrible, but why should you people at home not know? The horror was indescribable . . . I want to tell you so that it may be on record, that I honestly believe that Goldie (a mate) and many others were murdered through the stupidity of those in authority.* ❞

FIELD MARSHAL HAIG: 'THE BUTCHER OF THE SOMME'?

Politicians, including members of the government, began to wonder whether Haig's approach was working. They accepted that the pressure had been taken off Verdun, but they were concerned about the number of dead and wounded.

> **SOURCE 12** A personal memoir written by Winston Churchill MP in August 1916
>
> 66 *I view with the utmost pain, this terrible killing of our troops. We have not gained in a month's fighting as much ground as we were expected to gain in the first two hours. We have not advanced two miles in a direct line at any point . . . Nor are we making for any point of military importance; it is all open country which can easily be defended by the use of trenches.* 99

> **SOURCE 13** A letter written to the *Daily Telegraph* by Lord Lansdowne, an ex-Cabinet Minister, on 29 November 1916
>
> 66 *We are slowly but surely killing off the best of the male population of these islands. Can we afford to go on paying the same sort of price for the same sort of gain?* 99

This celebrated letter became known as the Lansdowne Letter. It was the first time that a leading politician had openly questioned the way the War was being fought.

Major-General (addressing the men before practising an attack behind the lines). "I WANT YOU TO UNDERSTAND THAT THERE IS A DIFFERENCE BETWEEN A REHEARSAL AND THE REAL THING. THERE ARE THREE ESSENTIAL DIFFERENCES: FIRST, THE ABSENCE OF THE ENEMY. Now (turning to the Regimental Sergeant-Major) WHAT IS THE SECOND DIFFERENCE?"
Sergeant-Major. "THE ABSENCE OF THE GENERAL, SIR."

SOURCE 14 A cartoon from *Punch* magazine

> ## Activity
>
> It is 1916. You have seen the cartoon in Source 14. Write a letter to the magazine in response to the cartoon. Your letter should either support or complain about the way the generals are fighting the War.

Did Haig make mistakes?

SOURCE 15 Judgements on Haig

> 1. Source 15 gives some judgements on Haig's leadership. Can you match each sentence up to the character who you think might have said it?

1967 The historian Sir Llewellyn Woodward

1919 Lovat Fraser, a fighting soldier

1922 Colonel J.H. Boraston. He was Haig's personal secretary during the War

1968 Field Marshal Montgomery, who was one of Britain's army chiefs in World War II

It may seem to you that Haig was silly, ignorant or uncaring. The costly tactics used at the Somme were used again and again until the final breakthrough in 1918. But historians have to try to look at things from the perspective of people at the time. For example, Source 17 was written by Haig himself, to explain his tactics, while Source 16 was written by a modern historian.

SOURCE 16 From a book called *Field Marshal Haig*, written by the historian Philip Warner in 1991

66 *If the criterion of a successful general is to win wars, Haig must be judged a success. The cost of victory was appalling, but Haig's military methods were in line with the ideas of the time, when attrition was the method all sides used to achieve victory.*

The full horrors of the First World War make it difficult to reach a clear appraisal of Haig. Those who admit he did eventually push the most powerful army in the world off French soil criticise the cost of the way he did it without offering alternative methods. 99

Our High Command had not advanced beyond the tactics of the Stone Age. They could not think of any other form of warfare, except to throw into battle large numbers of men month after month.

The Battle of the Somme was a great triumph for the genius of British leadership.

Haig's method of winning the War was clumsy, expensive in loss of life, and based on a misreading of the facts.

Haig was unimaginative and dull. Nothing can excuse the casualties of the Somme.

SOURCE 17 Haig's own explanations for his tactics, all written just after the War in 1919

66 ■ *In the course of the struggle, losses are bound to be heavy on both sides, for in this the price of victory is paid. There is no way of avoiding this . . . but our total losses in this war have been no larger than were to be expected.*
■ *We attacked whenever possible, because a defensive policy involves the loss of the initiative.*
■ *The object of all war is victory and a defensive attitude can never bring this about.* 99

In fact many historians have suggested ways in which Haig could have changed his tactics at the Battle of the Somme:
■ When he realised the full-frontal attacks were not breaking through, he could have stopped them. The Germans' advance had already been halted.
■ Haig could have attacked without bombardments, which always warned the Germans that an attack was coming and took away the surprise.
■ The British Navy could have been used to bomb the Germans from the west and Haig could have attacked the Germans' west flank close to the coast of Belgium.
■ Instead of vast waves of infantry going over the top, flexible teams of machine gunners could have been used to attack the weak points in the German trench system without massive loss of life.

---

2. Choose one statement from Sources 15 and 17 that you agree with and one that you disagree with. Explain your choice.
3. Why do you think Haig did not choose any of the options above? Sources 16 and 17 may help.
4. Why do you think there is so much disagreement about Haig?

Activity

It is the anniversary of the Battle of the Somme. You have been asked to make a short radio feature to explain:
■ what happened at the Battle of the Somme
■ whether Haig made mistakes or whether he simply did a difficult job in a difficult situation.

Get into groups and make a feature about five minutes long.

Animals at war

THROUGHOUT the War animals played an important part in the operations of every side. The world might have entered the age of the car, the motorcycle and the radio, but in trench warfare, horses, dogs and pigeons were often more effective to transport goods or carry messages.

Horses

In almost every war until the First World War, the cavalry had been a most important weapon. Field Marshal Haig had used cavalry with great success in the last war Britain had fought, on the wide, open plains of Southern Africa. At the start of the War both Britain and Germany had a cavalry force of over 100,000 and each side's generals believed it would be vital for winning battles. Source 1 shows the theory. Throughout the War, patriotic magazines carried such images of courageous cavalry charges.

The reality was very different. The mud, the barbed wire and the deadly machine-gun fire of the Western Front made a cavalry charge impossible. When it was tried the slaughter was awful. For example, in a cavalry attack on 30 March 1918, only four out of 150 horses survived the charge against the German machine guns.

But although the cavalry charge was a thing of the past the horse was not. Horses proved their worth again and again on the Western Front, even though the work they did was never easy.

More than two and a half million horses and mules were treated in veterinary hospitals in France during the War. Nearly two million were cured and returned to duty.

More than eight million horses died on all sides between 1914 and 1918: 484,143 were from Britain according to official figures.

SOURCE 2 A horse and water cart stuck in mud at Ypres, August 1917

SOURCE 3 Written by a Royal Artillery officer

The vet insisted Sailor was too old, too thin and unfit for service. He didn't know. He only judged by appearances. Sailor wasn't much to look at, but was worth six horses in the battery [gun team]. If a gun team jibbed [got stuck], we hitched up old Sailor and he pulled them through. If a vehicle got stuck in a ditch, or was too heavy to start, old Sailor moved it. He would work for 24 hours without winking. He was quiet as a lamb and as clever as a thoroughbred, but he looked like nothing on earth, so we lost him. The whole battery kissed him goodbye and the drivers and gunners who fed him nearly cried.

SOURCE 4 From an account by Private Sydney Smith in 1917

I had the terrible experience to witness three horses and six men disappear completely under the mud. It was a sight that will live for ever in my memory; the cries of the trapped soldiers were indescribable as they struggled to free themselves. The last horse went to a muddy grave, keeping his nostrils above the slush until the last second. A spurt of mud told me it was all over.

SOURCE 1
A cavalry charge pictured in *The Great War* – a weekly magazine published in Britain throughout the War

1. Look at Sources 2 and 3. Why do you think they used horses for these jobs?
2. Do you consider the deaths of millions of horses to be acceptable?

Dogs

Communication between the front line and the headquarters was a real problem in the Great War. Artillery BATTERIES were often positioned a kilometre behind the front line, and the generals were many more kilometres behind them. Communication between the artillery and the front line was essential: otherwise, the guns could easily end up pounding their own front lines.

Various methods were used to get messages through. But they all had drawbacks. Telegraph wires could be broken by shell fire. Radio messages were very unreliable and could be intercepted at the front line by the enemy, who were only a few hundred metres away. Human messages – even taken by bicycle – were too slow. Motor transport was often unusable where roads had been churned up into rubble and mud by constant shelling followed by rain. What was the solution?

> **SOURCE 5** Colonel Edwin Richardson, a retired army officer, trained dogs for war service at a training school in Scotland. This is a report about two of his Airedale terriers called Wolf and Prince
>
> *During the operations against the Germans, two messenger dogs belonging to this brigade were sent forward at 1.00 a.m. They were attached to front-line officers.*
>
> *After the artillery attack had finished, they were sent back, one at 10.45 a.m. and the other at 12.45 p.m. Both dogs reached Brigade HQ, travelling a distance as the crow flies of 4000 yards [3657 metres] over ground they had never seen before and over very difficult land. The dog which left at 12.45 p.m. reached his destination in under the hour, bringing in an important message. This was the first message received, all other communication having failed.*

SOURCE 6 A messenger dog with burns on his paws caused by a poison gas attack in 1918

Pigeons

Pigeons were also used for sending messages. They turned out to be more reliable than field telegraphs, radios or despatch riders on bicycles. They were always sent in pairs – two males or two females – and could fly distances of up to 96 kilometres. Their success rate was high: 100,000 pigeons were used in the War and 95 per cent got through with their messages.

SOURCE 7 A poster displayed in Leeds in 1915

---

1. Why do you think dogs and pigeons were better at carrying messages than humans or technology?
2. Can you think of any big problems with using horses, dogs or pigeons on the Western Front?

The technology of war

THROUGH the last 20 pages there has been much talk of 'stalemate'. Let's recap what this is and why it happened in the War.

A stalemate occurs when the sides in a war are so evenly balanced that neither can make a decisive breakthrough against the enemy. This was the situation in trench warfare. The stalemate was largely the result of technology. Britain and Germany were the most technologically advanced countries in the world in 1914. Each side had developed such lethal killing machines that trenches were easy to defend. For example, a machine gun could mow down hundreds of men a minute as they charged towards a trench.

Artillery was still more deadly. For much of the War, all day, every day, (and through the night) massive guns would bombard the enemy trenches. Big guns could fire from long distances behind the front line, trapping the enemy in their trenches, wearing down their morale and destroying their supply lines. More soldiers were killed and injured by artillery fire, than by any other cause, even machine-gun fire. The shells also churned up the ground and left huge craters, making it hard for soldiers of either side to advance over No Man's Land.

Stalemate!

However, if modern technology had helped create the stalemate, then perhaps new or improved technology could help to overcome it. On pages 51–63 you will investigate technology in the air and the sea war. Here you are going to look at two technological developments that were supposed to create a breakthrough in trench warfare: poison gas and tanks.

Gas

At 5.30 p.m. on 22 April 1915, the Germans released about 152 tonnes of chlorine gas into the air above their trenches at Ypres. They allowed the gas to drift on the wind onto the British trenches about 200 metres away. The troops began to cough and retch and panic set in. This was the first gas attack of the First World War. It struck terror into the troops and from then on gas attacks were a fact of life in the trenches for the soldiers of both sides.

To start with, the aim of the attacks was to knock out the enemy soldiers so that your own could attack them more easily. But gradually more and more lethal gases were developed, which killed, blinded, maimed or blistered the enemy.

German, British and French scientists worked on new substances to attack the enemy and tried to perfect new gas masks to protect their own soldiers.

There were two ways of launching a gas attack. You could release the gas and let it be blown onto your enemy by the wind. Or you could pack it into shells and fire them at the enemy trenches. In any case, launching a gas attack was a very dangerous job. If the wind changed direction the gas could blow back into your own trench. Leaks from cylinders were common. And if a gas attack was followed up by your own troops attacking the enemy lines, they needed to be well protected with gas masks, which restricted their mobility and vision, and made breathing difficult.

---

1. Gas attacks are forbidden in modern warfare by the Geneva Protocol of 1925. Why do you think this is?
2. Do you think it is a sensible rule? Explain your answer.

SOURCE 1 British machine gunners wearing gas masks, 1916

SOURCE 3 Written by Captain A.F.P. Christison of the Cameron Highlanders

Friday 13 July 1917
It proved to be a bad day . . . at about 0800 hours, the Germans started shelling steadily. One shell landed in my trench almost beside me and did not burst. I felt a burning sensation just above my right knee and heard the man next to me retch and cough . . . I shouted 'Gas' and quickly put on my respirator. The gas alarm immediately sounded and as we were good at our gas drill, only five or six of my company were gassed.

Captain Rowan and his men had put on respirators, but after wearing them for some time in the heat of the morning and no attack developing, they thought the original warning had been false as no gas had been smelt. What they did not know was that this was mustard gas, had no smell and had delayed action. The C Company trenches were saturated with the stuff . . . By nightfall, every officer and man was either dead or in hospital.

Tanks

The most pressing problem if the stalemate was to be broken was how to overcome the enemy's machine guns. They could cut down whole companies of men in seconds. What was needed was a method of attack that did not expose men to machine-gun fire.

In October 1914 a proposal was presented to the British government. It sketched what mechanised warfare would be like. Armoured machines on caterpillar tracks would be brought into position at night. They would advance on the enemy, smashing obstructions on the way and would be protected from enemy machine guns by their armour. They would sweep enemy trenches with machine-gun fire. Behind them, foot-soldiers would advance in short rushes. The proposal said that surprise would be vital. Smoke screens might be used, so that the advance of the armoured vehicles would be hidden from the enemy.

The army rejected the plan. But one wartime minister, Winston Churchill, thought the idea could work. His navy department put money into the idea. After two years of trialling and designing, the first working armoured vehicles were ready. They were carried over on a ship to France on a cool summer's night in 1916. To disguise their invention from the German spies the British covered the armoured vehicles and labelled them 'Water tanks'. The name stuck. From then on armoured vehicles were known as tanks.

SOURCE 4 A description of the inside of a tank from a school textbook, *Britain at War* by Craig Mair, published in 1982

The tanks carried a crew of about eight men. Conditions inside were terrible. The engine gave off strong fumes. It became so hot that the crew men wore leather jerkins to protect them when they were thrown against the hot moving parts as the tank lurched across the battlefield. The temperature inside could reach over 38 degrees Centigrade. The cramped and sweaty crew were quickly exhausted. The noise inside was so loud that the commander had to give orders by hand signals.

SOURCE 5 A photograph taken on 15 September 1916 at the village of Flers on the Somme. This was the first tank to be used in action

Tanks in action

Tanks were first used by Field Marshal Haig at the Battle of the Somme. It was a desperate attempt to gain something from the battle when the infantry was being slaughtered. The Germans were amazed. But there were not enough tanks to have a big effect; they were unreliable, and they only travelled at around ten kilometres per hour in any case. Worst of all, the great secret weapon was no longer a secret. From then on German positions were defended by anti-tank ditches.

SOURCE 8
A government poster of 1917

> **SOURCE 6** By a German war correspondent, 1916
>
> When the German lookouts crept out of their dugouts in the mist of the morning and stretched their necks to look for the English, their blood chilled! Mysterious monsters were crawling towards them over the craters . . . The monsters approached slowly, hobbling, rolling and rocking. Nothing stopped them . . . Someone in the trenches said 'The devil is coming', and the word was passed along the line. Tongues of flame leapt from the sides of the iron caterpillars . . . The English infantry came in waves behind.

> **SOURCE 7** Written by a British officer, Captain Lionel Ferguson, in 1917
>
> An enemy machine gun opened up on our right . . . and the old tank went right for it, firing a round of shot as it advanced. We stopped to watch the scrap . . . for all the world like a big dog going for a rat.
>
> The machine gun was firing the other way and before the Boche [German] gunners had time to escape, the huge monster was upon them, finishing them for ever.
>
> It was the first blood we had seen that morning and for us spectators, a most thrilling moment.

Tank design continued to improve and at the Battle of Cambrai in November 1917 it seemed that tanks might at last make a difference. At 6.20 a.m. on 20 November 1917, 378 British tanks smashed a giant hole ten kilometres wide in the German defences. By 4 p.m. they were six kilometres into German-held territory.

But then things started to go wrong. There were not enough infantry to follow up and this gave the Germans time to recover and fight back. Sixty-five tanks were destroyed by enemy shellfire and then, as the battle went on, over 100 ran out of petrol and were marooned in enemy territory. Having spent all day in their cramped compartments with gunsmoke and petrol fumes, the crews were exhausted. Many of them died trying to get back to their own lines.

The tank's time had not yet come, although you will see from page 82 that later in the final months of the War it would have a more decisive role to play.

---

1. Explain what impression Sources 6–8 give of the effectiveness of tanks.
2. How accurate an impression is this?

Activity

1. Copy and complete a chart like the one below.

	Strengths	**Weaknesses**
Gas		
Tanks		

2. Choose either gas or the tank and explain in your own words why it did not break the stalemate.

How important was the role of aircraft in the First World War?

THE aeroplane was a new weapon in the First World War. Today, we know what an important role aeroplanes can play in warfare. But when the War began, it had been only eleven years since the Wright brothers had made the first flight. General Foch, second in command of the French army in 1914, thought that aircraft were 'good for sport but useless for the army.' None of the countries that entered the First World War had many aircraft. So, how did the role of aircraft change during the War?

Some of the early planes were made of canvas and held together with piano wire. They were nicknamed 'stringbags'! They had no radios or parachutes, and their navigation was so limited that some of the aircraft failed to find their way back to base. This made night flying extremely dangerous.

SOURCE 1 An early British reconnaissance biplane

Reconnaissance

The main job done by these early aircraft was reconnaissance (finding out where the enemy troops are). They soon proved their worth: when cameras were fitted to aircraft it became possible to have very accurate aerial photographs of enemy positions.

Military commanders began to realise how valuable aircraft could be. In September 1914, at the Battle of the Marne, the Germans were on the verge of a breakthrough to Paris which could have won them the War. British aerial photographs showed a gap in the German lines that allowed British troops to advance, forcing the Germans to withdraw. Sir John French said that reconnaissance aircraft had given him information of 'incalculable value.'

1. Make a list of the dangers which the pilots of the early planes faced.
2. Why do you think the army commanders changed their minds about the value of aircraft as a weapon of war?
3. What do you think they would find useful in the photograph in Source 2?

SOURCE 2 This aerial photograph was taken on 19 July 1915 during preparations for the Battle of Loos in Belgium

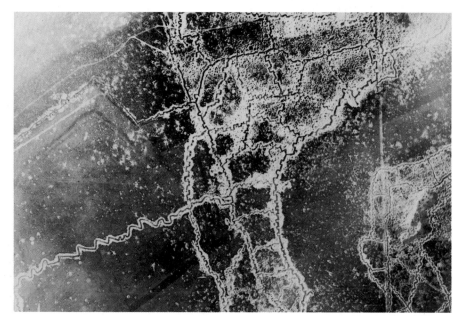

What impact did the War have on aircraft technology?

As the Western Front became 'bogged down' in trench warfare, it became more important to gain accurate information about the enemy's latest position so much better automatic cameras were developed. Each side tried to stop the other from gathering information, but at this time aircraft were not fitted with any weapons. All they could do was fire revolvers and rifles at each other as they flew along. This was not very effective so there was a demand for better weapons fitted into faster planes.

Better planes

The Germans were the first to invent a faster, more powerful aircraft. The British and French replied by producing an aircraft which made the previous machines OBSOLETE. Machine guns were SYNCHRONISED with the propeller blades so that the pilot could fire the guns forward without shooting off the blades. Technicians speeded up the development of radios so that pilots could keep in touch with each other and their bases.

The advances in weapons brought about the growth of more specialised aircraft for different tasks. 'Fighters' were designed to shoot enemy planes out of the sky while 'bombers' dropped ever more deadly weapons on enemy targets.

SOURCE 3 The most famous British fighter plane, the Sopwith Camel; its pilots shot down 1294 enemy aircraft. It was extremely manoeuvrable: pilots said it could almost make right-angle turns

SOURCE 4 German planes used during the War:
  a) Gotha bomber type G.III
  b) Fokker Triplane, a fighter

Zeppelins, bombers and air defence

When war broke out, German ZEPPELINS (see Source 5) could travel higher and faster than planes and were much better suited to dropping bombs. Zeppelins made 50 bombing raids on Britain in the first two years of the War (see page 85).

The public were shocked and frightened. They demanded protection. This led to the development of better fighter aircraft, which were so successful at shooting down Zeppelins that eventually the Germans stopped using them.

German designers then began to produce the technology needed for more effective bombing raids. In June 1917, new Gotha G. IV twin-engined bombers raided London and killed or injured nearly 600 people. The public outcry after these raids forced the government to bring into operation better searchlights, balloons, anti-aircraft guns and Sopwith Camel fighters. As a result, seven out of nineteen Gotha bombers were shot down in the raid of 19 May 1918 and German air attacks on Britain stopped.

SOURCE 5 Before the War, Zeppelins had transported 35,000 people between German cities

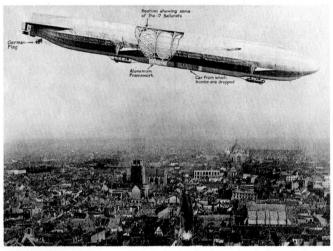

a

b

SOURCE 6
Aircraft development between 1914 and 1918

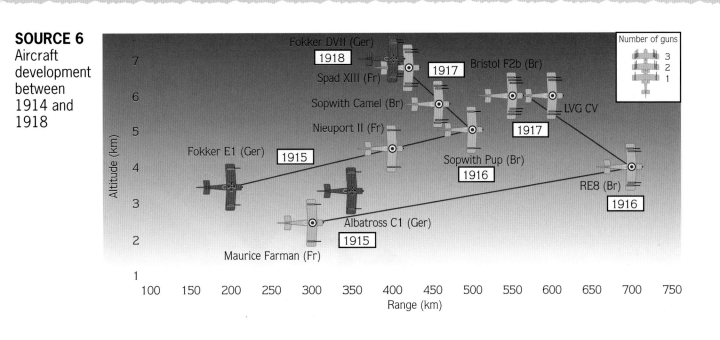

New uses and better facilities

The success of the aircraft in trench warfare encouraged the navy to use this new weapon against enemy submarines. This led to the building of aircraft carriers and to the first successful take-off from a ship. It also led to the development of flying boats and torpedoes that could be attached to aircraft.

By October 1918 there had been a huge increase in the size of the Royal Flying Corps (RFC) which now had 22,171 aircraft. This meant that facilities on the ground had to improve. Bigger and better hangars were needed to protect the new aircraft from the weather. Improvements in clothing and the development of oxygen equipment made life a little more comfortable for pilots.

1. Why do you think Zeppelins rather than planes were used for bombing in the first years of the War?

2. How did aircraft technology develop between 1914 and 1918? Copy and complete a chart like the one below.

	1914	1918
How far could planes fly?		
How high could planes fly?		
In what ways were planes thought to be useful to the war effort?		

3. Explain how some of these changes in air warfare technology were connected:
   - Reconnaissance aircraft
   - Aerial cameras
   - More powerful fighter aircraft
   - Machine guns synchronised with propeller blades
   - Zeppelin raids
   - New fighters
   - Gotha bombers
   - Air defence

4. What do you think were the main reasons for the changes in aircraft technology, 1914–18?

Aces

The developments in technology changed the nature of warfare in the skies. Fighter aircraft pursued and shot down enemy planes, pouncing on them from out of the sun and using any extra bit of speed or power to gain an advantage. The only method of defence was counter-attack, with planes circling round each other like dogs. Therefore, these battles between aircraft became known as 'dogfights'.

These heroic fights, almost like knights jousting in the Middle Ages, captured the imagination of the public. Sudden-death encounters, high above the trenches, made exciting stories for the newspapers, weary of reports of mass slaughter on the Western Front. The success or failure of their fighter planes had a great effect on British and German morale. This was much more significant than the actual impact of the aircraft on the War itself.

If you shot down five enemy planes, you became an 'ace' pilot, and air aces became immediate heroes. Perhaps the most famous was the German pilot Manfred von Richthofen, the Red Baron, who claimed 80 enemy kills. Amongst British aces were Captain Albert Ball (43 kills) and Major Edward Mannock (over 50 kills) who was regarded as the greatest RFC patrol leader of the War, flying 200 SORTIES against the enemy.

SOURCE 7 A photo claiming to show a First World War dogfight. It is likely that it is a photo montage put together from a number of other photographs

SOURCE 8 An account written in 1978 by Lieutenant Ralph Silk, an observer in the Reconnaissance Squadron, 24 October 1918

66 *I had already made two flights over the enemy's lines that day, bombing, straffing [machine gunning] and taking photographs. I had retired to my tent for a rest when the Squadron Commander lifted the tent flap and said, 'Silk, you will have to go up again. The Huns [Germans] are withdrawing their guns on Le Cateau road. I want you to blast the lot' . . . I shook hands with him and rushed over to the waiting machine.*

Over the lines, a number of enemy Fokker machines swooped out of the sun upon our four RE8 machines, the air was full of wings and bullets. When my machine gave a lurch, I turned my head to my pilot, he had slumped over the controls mortally wounded. Next, I had a gunshot wound in the head. The machine went into a spin and finally crashed upon some trees near Le Cateau. I can faintly remember being lowered to the ground, then passed out. 99

SOURCE 9 Albert Ball was the first great air force hero of the British public. He shot down 43 enemy aircraft before he was killed at the age of 20. It was partly the fact that he was so young that endeared him to the public. His main fighting tactic was to dive underneath enemy planes and shoot them from below

▶ **SOURCE 10** *The Last Fight of Captain Ball – 17 May 1917*, a painting by Norman Arnold

SOURCE 11 Baron Manfred von Richthofen was called the Red Baron because his plane was painted red. He flew with a group of German flyers who painted their planes bright colours, becoming known as the Flying Circus. Killed at the age of 26, his death is something of a mystery. At the time it was claimed he was shot down by a Canadian pilot, but recent evidence suggests he was shot by an Australian soldier as he swooped low over the ground. A British soldier wrote in a letter that when he ran up to the German's plane, which had landed behind British lines, von Richthofen gasped, 'War es kaput' before dying

1. How do Sources 7 and 10 explain why aircraft pilots were called 'knights of the air'?
2. Does Source 8 support this image of how aircraft fought?
3. a) Are the paintings in Sources 7 and 10 useful evidence in telling us what dogfights were really like?
   b) How do you think they come to be painted?
4. a) Why do you think aircraft pilots became such heroes and were important to public morale?
   b) Why was this more important than their impact on the actual fighting of the War?

1. You are a war correspondent. Use the sources to write a report for your newspaper about seeing an aerial dogfight over the trenches. You wish to help the British war effort, so make your report as exciting and patriotic as you can. Alternatively, you could do it from a German viewpoint writing about the Red Baron.
2. Think about the way you wrote your report. In what ways (including language chosen) did you make it more patriotic? What does this suggest about the problems of using newspaper wartime reports as historical evidence?

'Biggles'

We often get our impression of what happened in the past from fictional books and films. Royal Flying Corps pilots of the First World War are usually presented as devil-may-care adventurers who acted in a gentlemanly manner towards their enemies. One of the most famous pilots in British fiction is Captain James Bigglesworth, known as 'Biggles'.

SOURCE 12 Captain W.E. Johns, in the introduction to *The Bumper Biggles Book*, 1983

66 *Many of the adventures that are ascribed to Biggles did actually occur, and are true in their essential facts. Students of air history may identify them . . . in the air at least, truth is stranger than fiction . . .*

Almost everybody has heard the story of Boelike, the German ace, of how he once found a British machine with a dead crew flying a ghostly course amid the clouds. On another occasion he shot down an F.E., which spinning viciously, threw its observer out behind the German lines and the pilot behind the British lines.

. . . Madon, another ace, once attacked a German two-seater at point-blank range – his usual method. A bullet struck the goggles off the Boche [German] observer and sent them whirling into the air; Madon caught them on his wires and brought them home. 99

Discussion

1. a) What impression of Biggles and the Germans is given by the extract in Source 13?
   b) What words and phrases help create this image?
2. Do you think stories like those about Biggles shape our idea of the history of the War? If so, how?
3. Does the information on pages 54–55 support Captain W. E. Johns, who flew in the First World War, that the stories of Biggles are not far from the truth (Source 12)?

SOURCE 13 Extract from *Biggles, Pioneer Air Fighter*, 1932

[The Germans had used a decoy plane, a Rumpler, to lure a young British pilot into a deadly trap. The pilot had just managed to get back to base and land his plane.]

66 *Biggles caught his breath as he saw the ugly red stain on his hand that had supported the wounded pilot's back.*

'How did they get you, kid?' he choked . . .

'My own fault,' he whispered faintly . . . 'I went down – after Rumpler . . . Thought I'd – be – clever.'

He smiled wanly [weakly].

'Albatrosses [German planes] waiting upstairs. It was a trap. They got me – Biggles. I'm going topsides. It's getting dark early, where are you – Biggles?' . . .

'Get that Rumpler – for me Biggles.'

'I'll get him, Batty; I'll get the swine, never fear,' replied Biggles, his lips trembling.

[Biggles found the decoy plane and the German Albatrosses waiting high above to set another trap for an unsuspecting British pilot. He climbed above them.]

'So there you are,' he muttered grimly. 'How many? One – two – three – four – five – six – seven. Ought to be enough for a solitary Camel [British plane] . . .'

[He dived his plane down through the German planes.]

'Come on, you swine,' he rasped through set teeth, and went through the lower Albatrosses like a thunderbolt.

The Rumpler lay clear below. He took the machine in his sights but held his fire. Down, down, down – a noise like a thousand devils shrieking in his ears . . .

At 200 feet [60 metres] he pressed his triggers, and his lips parted in a mirthless smile as he saw the tracers making a straight line through the centre of the Boche machine. The observer leapt round and then sank slowly onto the floor of the cockpit. The nose of the Rumpler jerked upwards, an almost certain sign that the pilot had been hit.

[The German plane crashed and Biggles raced for home.] 99

Summary: how important was the role of aircraft in the First World War?

There is no doubt that the exploits of fighter aces made for exciting newspaper articles during the War. But did aircraft have any real impact on the War itself?

> **SOURCE 14** From 'The Experience of World War 1' by J.M. Winter, *Equinox*, 1988.
>
> A military historian explains that even by 1918 aircraft were still not thought to be a vital weapon of war
>
> 66 *Aerial forces of 1914–1918 never escaped from a junior role. Only Britain formed a separate and completely independent air force, elsewhere aerial forces remained under the control of navies and armies. Aircraft were lightly armed. They could not do enough damage to major military targets to affect the course of a battle in a major way. Large machines were too expensive to build in large numbers, could not carry a bomb load to fit their size and were mechanically unreliable. Neither political leaders nor senior military and naval officers were sufficiently air-minded to think that aircraft could be anything more than useful additions to land and sea warfare.* 99

> **SOURCE 15** R.C. Nesbit, writing in the *History of the RAF*, 1995
>
> 66 *In September 1918, two retreating Turkish armies were caught and subjected to low-level bombing and machine-gun attacks by aircraft, resulting in an appalling slaughter of soldiers who had little defence. The armies were destroyed as fighting units. Turkey had no option but to surrender the following month.* 99

> **1.** Look at Sources 14 and 15.
> a) Do their views of the importance of the role of the air force agree?
> b) Why do you think they disagree? Could both be true?

SOURCE 16 A British heavy bomber plane. Bombs came out through a sliding hatch in the base of the plane

SOURCE 17 Pilots from *The Standard History*. At the start of the War there were two branches of the air service – the RFC and the RNAS. They joined in 1918 to form the RAF

Activity
Use all the information on the war in the air (pages 51–57) to complete a chart like the one below.

Reasons why it could be said that the air force played a minor role in the War.	Reasons why it could be said that the air force played a very useful role in the War.

Why was control of the sea so important in the First World War?

THERE were no decisive sea battles during the First World War. In fact, there were very few battles at all. But this does not mean that the war at sea was unimportant. Some historians would say that the British navy played a vital role in defeating Germany.

Control of the sea was important to both sides. The British Isles depended on ships to bring in food, raw materials and other goods from abroad. Similarly, Germany needed to bring in supplies by ship to its northern ports. If either side controlled the sea, they hoped they could starve the other side into surrendering.

Both Britain and Germany had realised the importance of the sea before the War. British governments had spent vast sums of money to keep the navy ahead of the competition. In 1906 the British had launched a new type of battleship – the dreadnought. The Germans tried to build their own dreadnoughts. If you look back at the map on page 12 you can see Britain and Germany had the two most powerful navies in the world in 1914.

Despite this massive build up, Britain and Germany fought only one major naval battle during the War. This took place in May 1916 near Jutland in the North Sea (see page 62). Both sides claimed to have won the battle, but neither had delivered a knock-out blow to the enemy. The German fleet did not leave its base at Kiel again for the rest of the War.

One possible reason to explain why neither side was prepared to risk another big sea battle can be found in changes in technology.

Changes in sea-warfare technology

The dreadnought
A new type of battleship. It had huge guns (capable of firing over fourteen kilometres) and was very quick, making other battleships out of date. Other ships would not stand much chance if confronted by the guns of a dreadnought.

Guns
Improvements in guns were dramatic. In 1900 a battleship gun had a range of about 3650 metres. By 1914 it had increased to over 13,000 metres. Both sides had large guns, but the Germans had better rangefinders and so they were probably more accurate.

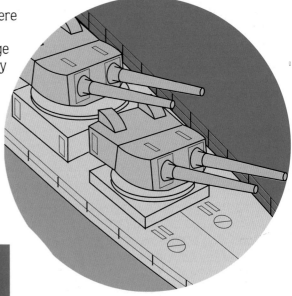

Torpedoes
This deadly weapon could hit a target eight kilometres away. During the War the technology improved so that a torpedo could be launched from ships, submarines or from the air. Both sides had torpedoes.

Mines

Both sides had powerful mines which could do great damage to enemy ships.

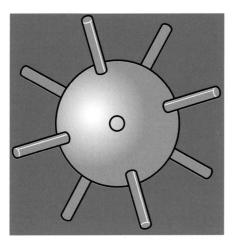

Aircraft carriers

In 1917 a British 'Sopwith Pup' made the first landing at sea on an aircraft carrier. Aircraft could be used for reconnaissance – to spy on the enemy beyond the horizon.

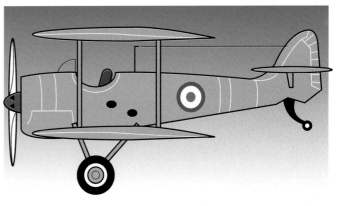

Radio

Improvements in radio meant that people could keep in better contact with each other and over longer distances than had been possible before.

Submarines

The submarine was a new weapon of war in 1914. Both sides had them but the Germans used them very effectively. New diesel engines allowed German U-boats (undersea boats) to travel greater distances and to stay away from port for weeks at a time.

Listening stations

Improvements in radio allowed British experts based at the top-secret 'Room 40' of naval intelligence to listen in to the enemy. When the British captured German codes it became difficult for the German navy to make a move without the British knowing about it.

1. Why did Britain need to control the seas around its shores?
2. What would happen if either Germany or Britain destroyed the navy of the other side in a sea battle?
3. Which of the changes in technology shown above do you think were most important in explaining why Britain and Germany did not want to fight a big sea battle? Explain your answer.

WHY WAS CONTROL OF THE SEA SO IMPORTANT IN THE FIRST WORLD WAR?

Who controlled the seas during the War?

Blockade

The main work of the British navy was in mounting a blockade to prevent ships taking goods to German ports. Source 1 shows how the British could stop German ships getting out into the North Sea. Ships sailing to neutral countries were searched, in case they carried supplies for Germany. The aim of this blockade was to weaken Germany by cutting off its supply of food and materials needed to keep the armed forces going.

By 1916 the blockade resulted in serious food riots in a number of German towns. Some Germans called the winter of 1916 the 'turnip winter' because turnips seemed to be about the only food that people could get to eat. German industry also began to run short of fuel and chemicals for explosives, as well as other supplies.

As the War went on, the blockade bit harder and harder. By 1918 thousands of Germans were starving and there was mutiny in the German navy. Some historians claim that the shortage of food and other goods caused by the blockade was one of the key factors in bringing about the German surrender. The main role of the British navy was enforcing the blockade and keeping German ships trapped in port. Although not very heroic in comparison with British naval battles of the past, it was certainly an extremely effective role.

U-boats

The British did not have everything their own way. The Germans fought back by using U-boats to get past the blockade and into the Atlantic. There they sank ships which were bringing goods to Britain from its Empire and from its most important supplier – the USA.

Proof of the power of the U-boats came in May 1915 when a U-boat sank a British liner, the *Lusitania*. A total of 1198 passengers died, including 128 US citizens. There were angry protests from the Americans, who were then still neutral in the War. The Kaiser ordered the German navy to stop attacking American ships because he did not want the USA, the richest country in the world, to enter the War on the allied side.

SOURCE 1 Map showing British blockade

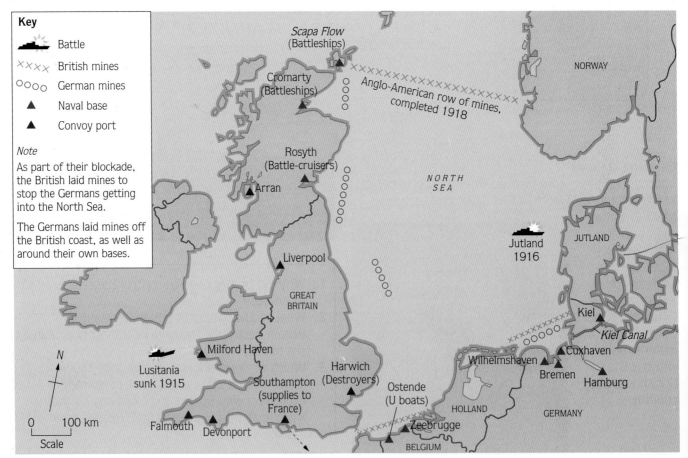

Unrestricted submarine warfare

By early 1917 the Germans were so desperate that they began attacking American ships again. This policy of unrestricted submarine warfare was a gamble – the Germans knew that it would bring the USA into the War, but hoped that it would force the Allies to surrender before the American army arrived in Europe. There were signs that the plan was working: by May 1917 so many ships had been sunk that Britain was left with only six weeks' supply of certain goods.

Convoys

The gamble did not succeed. On 7 April 1917 the Americans entered the War and sent men and supplies to help the British and French. To make matters even worse for Germany, the British began to defend their ships against U-boats by introducing the convoy system. Slow-moving merchant ships, which previously had been easy targets for the U-boats, now sailed together in convoys, protected by fast-moving destroyers. Soon the amount of shipping destroyed by U-boats began to fall.

Technology and trickery

The job of the U-boats was made even harder when the British started to use more powerful depth charges, minefields and massive anti-submarine nets. New aircraft with longer range and better radio systems joined in the fight. The British also used 'Q' ships. These looked like ordinary cargo ships, but when a U-boat surfaced to sink them by shellfire (not wanting to waste a torpedo), their crew pulled away dummy crates to reveal powerful guns which they turned on the U-boat.

SOURCE 2 From *The British Experience of Enforcing Blockade: The Armed Merchant Cruisers in 1915*, Chris Page, 1996. A British historian weighs up the role of the Royal Navy in the War

To some, the performance of the Royal Navy was disappointing: the hoped-for and expected Trafalgar-like encounter with the German High Seas Fleet did not take place, and the results of the only major Fleet action, off Jutland in May 1916, seem to support the feeling of disappointment. Too little tends to be made of the major successes. These include maintaining sea communications with Britain's friends, enabling us to feed their people and import the materials necessary to carry on with the War. This involved a great struggle to defeat the U-boats. The navy transported millions of troops with tiny losses. But perhaps the navy's prime achievement was the enforcement of the naval blockade. There is little doubt that it was a vital factor in the defeat of Germany.

SOURCE 3 A British destroyer escorting a convoy of ships

1. Give the meaning of the following: blockade, U-boat, unrestricted submarine warfare, convoy.
2. Look at Source 1. How did the British manage to keep the German navy from escaping into the North Sea and the Atlantic Ocean?

The Battle of Jutland, 1916

On May 31 1916 the only major sea battle of the War began (see Source 4). The German fleet, led by Admiral Scheer, had new dreadnoughts and modern battle-cruisers. The British Grand Fleet consisted of two forces – battle-cruisers and smaller ships under Admiral Beatty and dreadnoughts under Admiral Jellicoe. Beatty arrived first because his ships were faster and he was nearer.

When the battle started, it soon became clear that the Germans could fire their guns more accurately and that there was something seriously wrong with the British ships. The armour plating on the gun turrets was too thin, which meant that they were easily destroyed by direct hits (see Source 5). Two British ships blew up and Beatty was in trouble. The British ships held out as the battle raged, each side firing their guns through clouds of smoke and flashes.

Then, in the nick of time, Jellicoe arrived with his fleet of dreadnoughts and opened fire. The Germans now began to take more hits themselves, but they continued to inflict heavy damage on the British ships. Having done well, the German ships turned for home as night began to fall. German destroyers threatened to mount a torpedo attack on Jellicoe's ships so he did not chase them until it was too late. During the night there was more fighting as the two sides came close to each other, but by the time morning came the Germans had escaped safely back to port.

Who won?

The British lost fourteen ships and 6000 sailors. The Germans lost thirteen ships and 2500 sailors.

The Germans did better in the battle because the British ships lost were larger and more significant. But after Jutland, the German fleet never came out to fight again. It remained trapped in port and the British controlled the sea for the rest of the War.

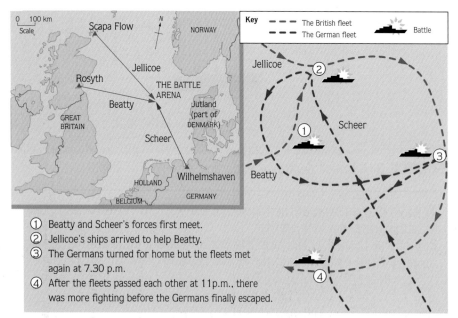

① Beatty and Scheer's forces first meet.
② Jellicoe's ships arrived to help Beatty.
③ The Germans turned for home but the fleets met again at 7.30 p.m.
④ After the fleets passed each other at 11p.m., there was more fighting before the Germans finally escaped.

SOURCE 4 Map showing Battle of Jutland

SOURCE 5 A young lieutenant on Beatty's own ship, *Lion*, wrote about the problem of the gun turrets

66 *. . . a bloodstained Sergeant of Marines appeared on the bridge. He was hatless, his clothes were burnt and he seemed somewhat dazed. I asked him what was the matter; in a tired voice he replied: '"Q" turret has gone, sir. All the crew are killed, and we have flooded the magazine.'*

I looked over the bridge. The armoured roof of "Q" turret had been folded back like an open sardine tin, thick yellow smoke was rolling up in clouds from the gaping holes and the guns were cocked up awkwardly in the air. 99

---

1. What problems did the British ships face in the Battle of Jutland?
2. Why might Admiral Jellicoe:
a) have had difficulty in persuading people he had won the battle in 1916?
b) have been able to claim that he had won after the War had finished in 1918?

Activity

Look back over the information on pages 58–62 and draw up two lists:

a) evidence which suggests that Britain 'won' the war at sea
b) evidence which suggests that Britain's control of the seas – the blockade and fighting the U-boat menace – was crucial in winning the War.

1 You know, I don't really think the air force made much difference at all – a few bombs here and there. That's nothing compared to the movement of thousands of troops. Airplanes were just a pinprick on the edges of the War.

2 I don't think you should take that attitude, old bean. Our reconnaissance planes took a lot of risks to get photographs of the warfront. We saved your bacon at the Battle of the Marne – told you exactly where the Germans were. You wouldn't have liked it if German planes had been flying over our trenches, dropping bombs. In the Middle East our bombing and straffing of the enemy were crucial.

3 Admit it, you're just jealous because the public made our pilots heroes – helped morale no end and that's important.

1 What did the navy do? You only got involved in one real battle. The rest of the War you spent in port. Nice life for some!

2 You don't just have to fight battles to win wars. Battles didn't seem to get you army types anywhere before 1918. We won the War for you. We brought the Germans to their knees by blockading their ports. They were starving and running out of crucial supplies by 1918.

3 Don't forget that we kept the seas open. We stopped German ships from raiding our coasts and kept supplies rolling in. And it wasn't easy fighting submarines you couldn't see. Defeating the U-boat menace was vital to winning the War.

Review Activity

How important were the Royal Flying Corps and the British navy in the War?

Write your own conclusions about the importance of the air force and the navy in the War. Use the statements above and what you have learned from the sections on the war in the air and at sea. Weigh up the various factors in terms of the 'big picture' of the War – how much the navy and air force contributed to the War as a whole.

Mention:
- the usefulness of aircraft in the War
- how powerful aircraft weapons were and what difference these weapons made to battles and large armies
- the result of the main naval battle at Jutland
- the effects of the British naval blockade
- the role of the navy in keeping the seas open.

In your final conclusion, decide whether you think the navy or the air force played a more important role in defeating the Germans.

63

Theatres of war

YOU HAVE already studied trench warfare on the Western Front in France. But the War was going on in other parts of Europe and in other parts of the world. This is why it is called the First WORLD War.

As you can see on the map, the major fronts were in Europe, although there was significant fighting in the Middle East. More distant parts of the world were also involved. Germany had colonies and territory in different parts of Africa. The British used Empire troops – Indians, South Africans, West Indians and Nigerians – to take control of these. But there was a long struggle throughout the War in German East Africa (now Tanzania). The Japanese, allies of the British, seized German territory in China.

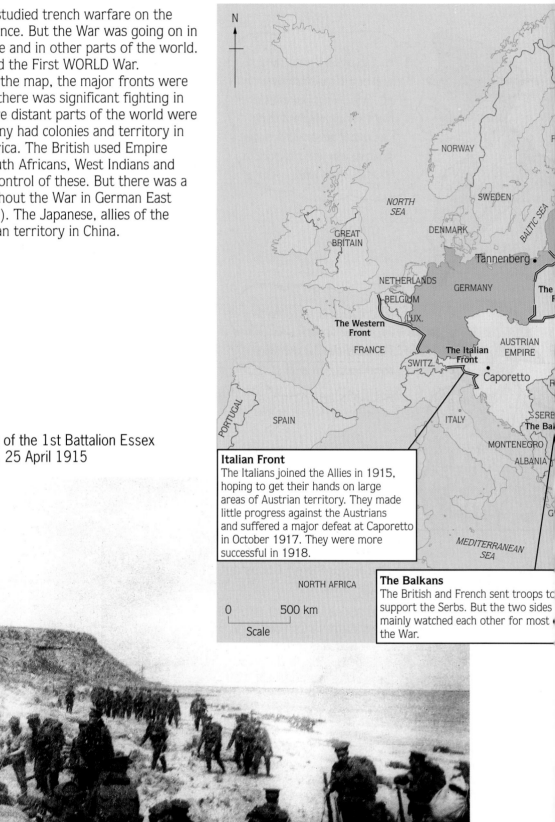

SOURCE 1 Landing of the 1st Battalion Essex Regiment at Gallipoli, 25 April 1915

Italian Front
The Italians joined the Allies in 1915, hoping to get their hands on large areas of Austrian territory. They made little progress against the Austrians and suffered a major defeat at Caporetto in October 1917. They were more successful in 1918.

The Balkans
The British and French sent troops to support the Serbs. But the two sides mainly watched each other for most of the War.

The Western Front

The Italian Front

Eastern Front

The Russians fought the Germans and the Austrians on a long front stretching from the Baltic Sea to the Black Sea. For most of 1914 and 1915 the Russians were in retreat although they mounted a very successful offensive in 1916. The fighting stopped after the Communists took over Russia in the revolution of November 1917.

Key

→ Allied attacks and advances

Gallipoli

The Allies, with many soldiers from Australia and New Zealand, made a bold attempt to knock Turkey out of the War by capturing Constantinople (the old name for Istanbul) and the sea straits linking the Mediterranean to the Black Sea. However, the landings on the Gallipoli peninsula were a total disaster.

The Middle East

When Turkey joined the War on Germany's side, the British sent forces to protect their oil supplies in Mesopotamia and their supply routes to the East, especially the Suez Canal. In Palestine, British, Australian, New Zealand and Indian troops, working with Arab forces, drove the Turkish army back towards Turkey itself. In Mesopotamia the Allies pushed the Turks back, seizing control of Basra and Baghdad.

RUSSIA

The Eastern Front

BLACK SEA

TURKISH EMPIRE

poli

Baghdad

Tigris

Euphrates

Damascus

PALESTINE

MEDITERRANEAN SEA

PERSIAN GULF

EGYPT

Aqaba

ARABIA

How were the fronts related?

We must not think that these fronts were unrelated. The Eastern Front in particular had a major effect on what was happening in the west. If the Germans had not been forced to split their forces to fight on the Western and Eastern Fronts at the same time, they might have won the War. On two important occasions when their positions on the Western Front were in danger, Britain and France asked the Russians to attack so that the Germans had to withdraw troops and send them to the east.

Gallipoli, the Balkan Front and the Italian Front were all attempts to break the stalemate on the Western Front. The Allies were trying to find other routes by which they could attack the Germans and Austrians since they had failed to break through in the west.

SOURCE 2 Arab patrol in the Middle East

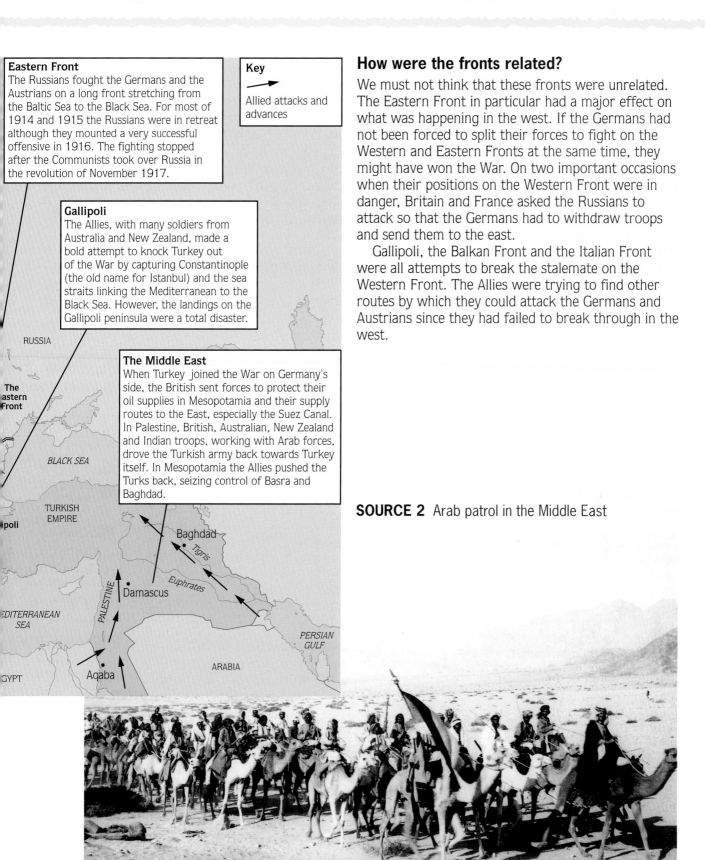

Was it worth taking the gamble at Gallipoli?

BY THE end of 1914 it became clear to the British that it would be very difficult to break through German trench defences on the Western Front – there was a complete stalemate. Early in 1915 the Russians on the Eastern Front were coming under increasing pressure. The War Council in Britain was worried that if the Germans beat the Russians on the Eastern Front, then huge numbers of German troops could be moved to fight on the Western Front.

Winston Churchill put forward a plan to break the stalemate and help the Russians. His plan was to attack Constantinople (now called Istanbul) and deal Turkey, Germany's ally, a blow that would put it out of the War.

Allied troops were to be landed on a part of Turkey known as the Gallipoli peninsula. They would capture the Turkish forts that controlled the Dardanelles and then make their way overland to capture Constantinople. Meanwhile the navy would sail through the Dardanelles to attack from the sea (see Source 1). The War Cabinet decided to go ahead with the plan.

A BOLD PLAN . . .

- It could knock Turkey out of the War.
- An army could be sent to attack Austria on a new front and take pressure off the Russians.
- Control of the Dardanelles and the Bosphorus (two narrow straits of water that formed a link between the Mediterranean and the Black Sea) would allow allied ships to transport war supplies to the desperate Russians. This would keep the Eastern Front open.
- It could bring the War to an end quickly.

. . . BUT

- Lord Fisher, the First Sea Lord did not want to send his best ships because he thought they would be needed against the Germans in the Baltic. He was worried that any ships he sent would be sunk by Turkish guns or German submarines and mines.
- Lord Kitchener was reluctant to send troops and supplies that he thought would be needed on the Western Front. He also did not want to send his best officers.
- The Allies didn't really know how many troops the Turks had to defend Gallipoli.

SOURCE 1 Map of Gallipoli and surrounding area

BLACK SEA

BULGARIA

The Dardanelles and the Bosporus linked the Mediterranean to the Black Sea. Turkish forts had heavy guns trained on the straits so that allied ships could not sail through.

To RUSSIA

Constantinople — Bosporus

All of the Gallipoli beaches were in range of Turkish gunners.

SEA OF MARMARA

Gallipoli

Dardanelles

TURKISH EMPIRE

MEDITERRANEAN SEA

N

0 — 200 km
Scale

Supply problems
- Supplies had to be brought in from British bases in Egypt, which was 600 miles away.
- Britain was 3000 miles away; Australia 7000 miles.

Key
- Ground captured in April
- Ground captured at Suvla Bay in August
- Turkish fort, with large guns
- Turkish mines
- Allies

Suvla Bay
Aug. 1915

Anzac Cove
April 1915

Gallipoli

Y
X
S
Allied naval attack. March

Cape Helles
W V

N

0 — 3 km
Scale

The commanders

▼ SOURCE 2 Liman von Sanders (1855–1929), was a German officer who had been sent to Turkey in 1913. He helped reorganise the Turkish forces and in 1915 became the new commander of the Turkish Fifth Army. He organised the defence of the Gallipoli peninsula against the threat of allied landings

◄ SOURCE 3 Sir Ian Hamilton (1853–1947), had had a long and successful army career before the Gallipoli campaign. He had been an officer in the Boer War, 1899–1902. In 1915 he was appointed to lead the allied forces in the Gallipoli campaign

Setting off for Gallipoli

Many of the troops who were to take part in the Gallipoli campaign were ANZAC troops (from Australia and New Zealand). Soon after Britain declared war on Germany, the Australians promised to help the British. An army of 20,000 volunteers was raised quickly. It was called the Australian Imperial Force (AIF). The level of training and army experience was low, but the troops were tough and brave. The New Zealanders already had a well-trained army of 30,000 men.

When the British troops set off for Gallipoli there was a mood of great confidence. Historians think that one reason for this confidence was that the British thought the Turks were not good soldiers and that their army was poorly organised. Churchill was convinced that Constantinople could be taken in three weeks. He was sure the navy would do severe damage to the Turkish forts and the allied troops would easily overwhelm the Turks.

Activity

1. Use all the information and sources for this Activity. Draw a chart like the one below.

Gallipoli was a gamble worth taking	Gallipoli was not likely to succeed

On the left-hand side put:
a) all the reasons why Gallipoli was thought to be such a good plan
b) why the Allies were confident of winning.

On the right-hand side put:
a) the reasons why Gallipoli was a difficult place to attack (see Source 1)
b) other factors working against the success of the plan.

2. Divide the class into two sides. One side should argue that Gallipoli was a great opportunity to end the War quickly. The other should argue that the risks were too great and there were too many factors working against the success of the plan.

3. Weigh up the pros and cons of the Gallipoli campaign. Would you have taken the gamble? Explain your answer.

WAS IT WORTH TAKING THE GAMBLE AT GALLIPOLI?

What happened at Gallipoli?

On 18 March 1915 a fleet of British battleships sailed into the Dardanelles and attacked the Turkish forts that lined the straits. Three British ships were sunk and little was achieved. Worse than this, it put the Turkish forces on alert to expect a land attack.

The landings

Just over a month later, on 25 April, British forces landed at five beaches at Cape Helles, while the Australian and New Zealand troops landed at a bay further north. This later became known as Anzac Cove. The plan was that the forces would quickly move inland and capture the forts before the Turkish forces could respond.

But when the troops landed on the beaches they found that their officers were not clear about what action to take. On one beach there were no Turkish defenders to be seen, but the troops had to wait for instructions. By the time they were ready to move inland, enemy forces had arrived and it was too late.

It was a similar story on three of the other beaches although on these the allied forces had to overcome Turkish resistance. Instead of moving quickly, the British officers told their men to dig trenches and prepare for a Turkish attack. Meanwhile, Sir Ian Hamilton (allied commander) was in a battleship a long way from the beaches and so was unable to co-ordinate the attacking forces.

On the fifth beach the attacking forces found the Turks ready and waiting for them. As the troops came ashore, they were caught in a murderous hail of bullets. Many were killed in the water which turned red with blood. Those who did reach the beach were cut down as they ran for cover.

At Anzac Cove the Australian and New Zealand forces also faced a desperate situation. Coming ashore under heavy fire, they found that the beach was surrounded by high cliffs. This made getting off the beach extremely difficult and chaotic as the men, often cut off from their officers, tried to find different routes up the cliffs. Some did reach the top, overcoming defenders, but once again there were no clear orders to move inland. Turkish reinforcements arrived and the Anzac forces were pinned down.

Survival

The story of the Gallipoli campaign after this was one of survival in appalling conditions. Both sides dug into trenches, as on the Western Front, but these were very close to each other, sometimes only nine metres apart. The soldiers could hear the other side talking and any movement could be dangerous.

Matters got worse when the summer arrived. Water was short in the hot, dry conditions and there were masses of flies which covered everything – men and food and excreta in the latrines. It was not long before dysentery and other diseases broke out.

The Turks proved themselves to be brave and determined soldiers. They mounted ferocious mass attacks, only to be mown down by machine-gun fire. Because the trenches were so close, there was often desperate hand-to-hand fighting in confined spaces. At times there were so many dead creating such a terrible smell that ceasefires were held so that the bodies could be buried.

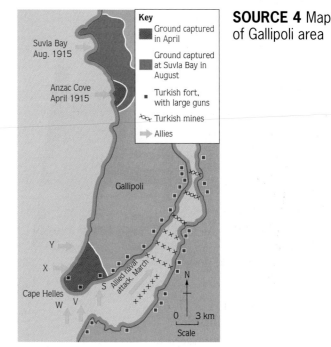

SOURCE 4 Map of Gallipoli area

Suvla Bay

In an attempt to break through, 2000 allied soldiers were to be landed on thinly defended beaches in or near Suvla Bay on 6 August. The troops would march six kilometres inland and occupy some low hills. From here they would join up with the Anzac troops and attack the Turks.

The plan went wrong. The 61-year-old General Stopford, who had not actually commanded any forces before, failed to order his troops to advance and capture the hills. He wasted the chance of making a decisive breakthrough. The Turks moved defenders to the area and both sides 'dug in' to a new round of trench warfare. After nine days Stopford was sacked. Eventually, in the winter of 1915, the troops were evacuated from Suvla and also from Anzac Cove and Cape Helles. The Gallipoli campaign had failed.

SOURCE 5 Memories from 2nd Lieutenant G.D. Horridge

❝After the battles of June 4 and 6, the land in between the trenches was covered with dead . . . Because of this and the hot sun, the flies bred there until their number was horrendous . . . They attacked our food remorselessly. Any bit of food uncovered was blotted out by flies in a couple of seconds. The contamination made everybody ill. Typhoid and dysentery were rife. Those that didn't get either had very unpleasant tummy trouble and were continually on the trot.❞

▲ **SOURCE 7** An Australian trench in the front line at Gallipoli. The Turkish trenches were only a few metres away. A sniper is using a clamped rifle and a sniperscope. Behind him another soldier is using a periscope to 'spot' enemy soldiers

SOURCE 6 Private Leonard Hart, Otago Infantry battalion, New Zealand

❝We were almost up to the firing line and the sight that presented itself is one I shall never forget. There were dead and wounded lying everywhere. The wounded were so numerous that it had been impossible to cope with them all and many had lain there for days . . . For the next few days there was little else but blazing away at the Turkish trenches to keep them quiet. We all learnt what real hunger and thirst were like.❞

◀ **SOURCE 8** An ambulance waggon stuck in mud after a storm, Gallipoli, November, 1915

1. What do you think was the major reason for the failure of the landings on the Gallipoli beaches?
2. Why did the Anzac soldiers find it so difficult to get off their beach?
3. What do Sources 5–8 reveal about conditions of the troops in the months after the landings?
4. Sources 5–6 are personal memories about Gallipoli. What are the advantages and disadvantages of such accounts as historical evidence?

Activity

Write a letter from a member of the Anzac forces to a relative back home. Tell the relative what happened when you landed, who you blame for it, and what conditions are like on the front line. Underline the parts that you think the censor might cut out of your letter.

Why was the Gallipoli campaign such a disaster?

There are many opinions about why the Gallipoli campaign was a disaster. Some people think it was doomed to failure from the beginning. Others think it could have been successful if there had been proper preparation and planning by senior officers, and if officers had been more committed and made the right decisions during the first attacks.

You have probably formed some of your own opinions after reading the last few pages. You are now going to reach some conclusions about the campaign.

Activity

1. Sources 9–15 on these pages give some reasons why the Gallipoli campaign failed. Read through the sources and complete a chart like the one below. You will need to draw a much larger copy for yourself.

Source	Reasons why the Gallipoli campaign failed

2. Use your chart and information from previous pages to write an essay on why the Gallipoli campaign failed. Use the diagram below to help you.

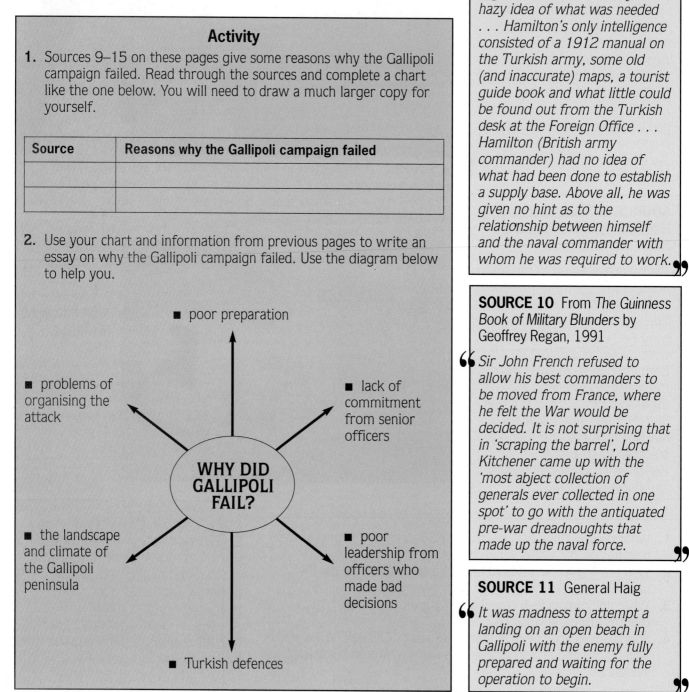

- poor preparation
- problems of organising the attack
- lack of commitment from senior officers
- the landscape and climate of the Gallipoli peninsula
- poor leadership from officers who made bad decisions
- Turkish defences

WHY DID GALLIPOLI FAIL?

SOURCE 9 From *Gallipoli* by Michael Hickey, 1995. A historian criticises the planning of the Gallipoli campaign

❝There was a lack of up to date knowledge about Turkish troop positions. The instructions were vague. Kitchener had only a hazy idea of what was needed . . . Hamilton's only intelligence consisted of a 1912 manual on the Turkish army, some old (and inaccurate) maps, a tourist guide book and what little could be found out from the Turkish desk at the Foreign Office . . . Hamilton (British army commander) had no idea of what had been done to establish a supply base. Above all, he was given no hint as to the relationship between himself and the naval commander with whom he was required to work.❞

SOURCE 10 From *The Guinness Book of Military Blunders* by Geoffrey Regan, 1991

❝Sir John French refused to allow his best commanders to be moved from France, where he felt the War would be decided. It is not surprising that in 'scraping the barrel', Lord Kitchener came up with the 'most abject collection of generals ever collected in one spot' to go with the antiquated pre-war dreadnoughts that made up the naval force.❞

SOURCE 11 General Haig

❝It was madness to attempt a landing on an open beach in Gallipoli with the enemy fully prepared and waiting for the operation to begin.❞

SOURCE 12 Sapper J. Johnson, 44th Welsh Field Company

66 *We were loaded into small boats and rowed towards the shores of Suvla Bay where we had to wade ashore for about sixty yards [55 metres] as the boats couldn't get in any nearer owing to the shallow water. The Turks had spotted the landing and opened up with fire. We were scared out of our wits. Then we began to look around for our officers for further orders, but there were no officers near us. It appeared that they had been landed further over from 'A' beach. We hung around all day waiting for orders. No one told us what to do so we stayed there all night.* 99

1. How can you tell from this photograph that Anzac Cove was a difficult place to attack?

SOURCE 13 Photograph taken at Anzac Cove, Gallipoli, after the allied landings, April 1915. On the hillside you can see some of the 'dugout' shelters built by the Anzac troops

SOURCE 14 Sir Maurice Hankey was the Cabinet secretary. He was sent to Gallipoli by the Prime Minister to give an honest report about the situation. This is from his report

66 *The only difficulty for the Turkish gunners is the great variety of targets – crowded beaches, horse lines, rest camps etc. The sun is intensely hot and there is no shade . . .*

What distressed me was the attitude of the officers. They were settling themselves in dugouts . . . They should have been making rough roads for the advance of the artillery and supply wagons, but instead they were making a huge system of trenches 'to protect headquarters'. It looked as if this accursed system of trench warfare in France had sunk so deep into our military system that all idea of attack had been killed. 99

SOURCE 15 From evidence given by Colonel Aspinall to the Commission of Enquiry into the failure of the Gallipoli campaign, 1917. Colonel Aspinall had gone to Suvla to assess the situation and went back to see Stopford to ask him to order the troops to advance

66 *'Well, Aspinall', beamed General Stopford, 'the men have done splendidly and been magnificent'.*

I was taken aback. 'But they haven't reached the hills, sir.'

'No,' replied Stopford, 'but they are ashore!'

All my arguments for an immediate advance were brushed aside by General Stopford. He answered that . . . 'until the men were rested and more guns and supplies were landed it was quite impossible to move.' 99

Why was there no breakthrough in the Balkans?

YOU WILL remember that the War started in July 1914 when the Austrians invaded Serbia (see pages 14–15). The Serbians fought back but they did not have much chance against the Austrians.

In October 1915 Britain and France sent troops to help the Serbs because they saw an opportunity to end the War quickly by breaking through the Balkans. They hoped to defeat the Austrians and send an army up through Austria–Hungary to attack the 'underbelly' of Germany. They hoped this would take pressure off the Russians on the Eastern Front and help the allied forces in Gallipoli who were, at the end of 1915, still bogged down in their trenches (see map, page 66).

SOURCE 2 From *Facing Armageddon*, H. Cecil and P. Liddle (eds.), 1996.

A historian argues that the British Prime Minister Lloyd George, who was the chief supporter of fighting a war in the Balkans, did not understand the problems

❝*Lloyd George's plan was not realistic. He ignored the jealousies and hatreds, created after the previous Balkan Wars, which made it impossible to unite the Balkan states against Germany and Austria. He ignored the fact that the engineers and building supplies needed to improve the Salonika railway line could only be obtained from the Western Front – where they were desperately needed. He forgot about how mountainous the country was. He forgot that the railway line would have been vulnerable to enemy raids unless protected by a fairly large force.*❞

1. Why did the Allies think that the Balkan Front was significant and would help them win the War?
2. Use Sources 1 and 2 to list the reasons why the British were unable to do much to help the Serbs and failed to make a breakthrough in the Balkans.

SOURCE 1 The war in the Balkans

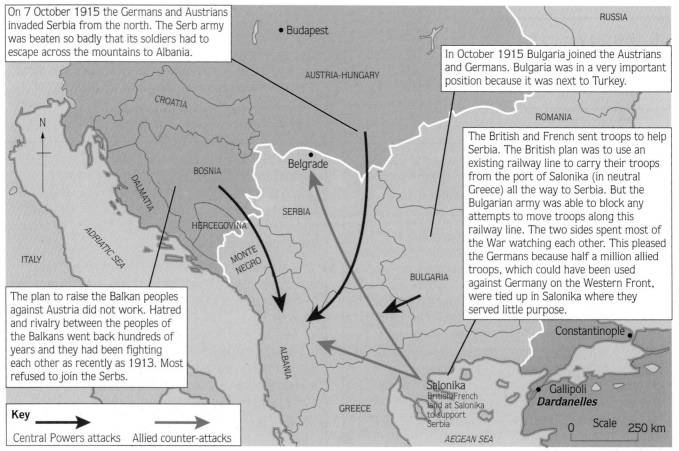

On 7 October 1915 the Germans and Austrians invaded Serbia from the north. The Serb army was beaten so badly that its soldiers had to escape across the mountains to Albania.

In October 1915 Bulgaria joined the Austrians and Germans. Bulgaria was in a very important position because it was next to Turkey.

The British and French sent troops to help Serbia. The British plan was to use an existing railway line to carry their troops from the port of Salonika (in neutral Greece) all the way to Serbia. But the Bulgarian army was able to block any attempts to move troops along this railway line. The two sides spent most of the War watching each other. This pleased the Germans because half a million allied troops, which could have been used against Germany on the Western Front, were tied up in Salonika where they served little purpose.

The plan to raise the Balkan peoples against Austria did not work. Hatred and rivalry between the peoples of the Balkans went back hundreds of years and they had been fighting each other as recently as 1913. Most refused to join the Serbs.

Key

→ Central Powers attacks   → Allied counter-attacks

How important was the campaign in the Middle East?

IN OCTOBER 1914 Turkey joined the War on Germany's side. Turkish control of the Black Sea threatened British supply routes to its Russian ally. In 1915 and 1916 Britain tried to force Turkey out of the War in the Gallipoli campaign but, as you know, this failed disastrously (see pages 66–71). However, the British had other concerns about the Turks whose Empire covered most of the Middle East.

The British feared that the Turks might try to close the Suez Canal and cut off Britain's sea routes to India, Australia and other parts of its Empire. The British also owned oil wells near Basra in Persia (modern Iran) and feared that the Turks might seize oil that was important to the war effort. So Britain sent armies to Egypt and Mesopotamia.

▶ **SOURCE 1** Map of Palestine campaign

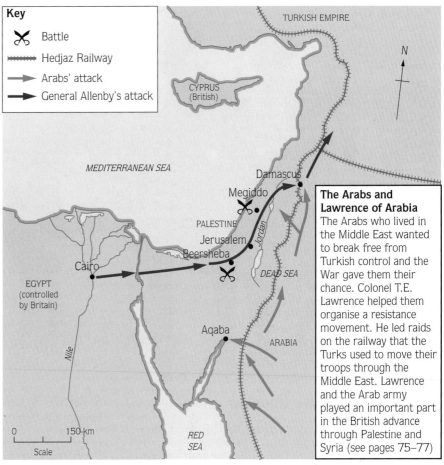

Key

✕ Battle
╫╫╫╫ Hedjaz Railway
➡ Arabs' attack
➡ General Allenby's attack

The Arabs and Lawrence of Arabia
The Arabs who lived in the Middle East wanted to break free from Turkish control and the War gave them their chance. Colonel T.E. Lawrence helped them organise a resistance movement. He led raids on the railway that the Turks used to move their troops through the Middle East. Lawrence and the Arab army played an important part in the British advance through Palestine and Syria (see pages 75–77)

The Palestine campaign

Australian, Indian and West Indian troops fought alongside British soldiers in Palestine and Syria. The British forces successfully defended the Suez Canal against an early attempt by the Turks to seize it in 1915. The Egyptian Expeditionary Force (EEF) then started to push their way out of Egypt and up into Palestine. General Allenby commanded the army, taking risks so that his forces did not get stuck in trench warfare. Allenby's troops captured Jerusalem in December 1917. In October 1918 they linked up with the Arab army, forcing the Turks out of Damascus and right back to Turkey.

▼ **SOURCE 2** The photograph shows Australian, Indian and British members of the Camel Corps. Troops faced incredible heat in the desert during the day and then found that the temperature dropped sharply at night

The Mesopotamian campaign

An enormous number of Indian troops – some 700,000 – fought alongside the British in Mesopotamia. In April 1916 the British and Indian troops were forced to surrender to the Turks at the siege of Kut. Despite this setback, by the end of the War, the Allies gained control of the rest of Mesopotamia, including Basra and Baghdad.

All troops found it very difficult to adapt to the desert conditions. Thousands died from fever and dysentery.

SOURCE 3 Indian soldiers of the 9th Hodson's Horse, serving in the British army, 1917

SOURCE 4 A historian looks at the problems of fighting in the Middle East

The Palestine and Mesopotamia campaigns were much more difficult to fight than the war in Europe. The desert war was fought across huge distances, making the job of supplying the troops a nightmare. In the summer season, supplies of drinking water had to be rationed. The land was hostile too. There were few landmarks and fewer reliable maps. Perhaps the biggest problem of all was the fact that the best equipment and weaponry were sent to the Western Front, leaving the armies in the Middle East to make do with antiquated weapons and shortage of supplies.

SOURCE 5 From *The Experience of World War 1*, by J.M. Winter, 1988. A historian assesses the importance of the Middle Eastern campaigns

The 'core' of the War remained in northwest Europe. Events in the 'periphery' [around the edges] were dramatic but indecisive. In the Middle East British forces captured Beersheba (October 1917), Jerusalem (December 1917) and Baghdad (March 1918), which helped weaken the Turkish Empire. None of these operations seriously shifted the balance of power in the War.

1. Why was the front in the Middle East so significant for the British and the war effort in general?
2. Why was it so difficult to fight a war in the Middle East?
3. What successes did the British have?
4. How important was the fighting in the Middle East? Do you think the writer in Source 5 is fair in his assessment?

Lawrence of Arabia

ONE OF the most fascinating characters to come out of the First World War was a young British officer called T.E. Lawrence, who became the legendary figure known as 'Lawrence of Arabia'. In this section we look at the story of how the Lawrence legend was created and the role Lawrence played in winning the campaign in the Middle East.

The Arab revolt

The Turks had ruled the Arabs in the Middle East for several centuries. When the War broke out, the Arabs seized their chance to break free of Turkish control. Encouraged by the British, the Arabs started a revolt in June 1916 and captured Mecca, their Holy City. But after this early success, they failed to take the important city of Medina and the Turks rushed men and supplies to the south. The revolt began to falter.

Enter Lawrence

Before the War T.E. Lawrence had been on archaeological expeditions to the Middle East where he spent several years living with the Arabs and becoming fluent in Arabic. In 1916 he was in Cairo using his expert knowledge in the Arab Bureau, a group set up to give the army advice on Arab affairs.

But Lawrence did not want a desk job. He went on a mission to meet the leaders of the Arab revolt. The British were looking for a charismatic Arab leader who could unite the Arab tribes. When Lawrence met Feisal, the third son of Sherif Hussein (an important Arab chieftan), he realised he had found the man who could do this. Lawrence returned to Cairo and recommended that the British support Feisal with weapons and supplies to make the Arab revolt successful. The British agreed.

The relationship with Feisal blossomed. The Arabs accepted Lawrence because he adopted their customs. Lawrence lived as an Arab – dressing, sleeping, eating, riding and walking barefoot in Arab style.

The taking of Aqaba

Lawrence and Feisal, with a small Arab army, seized control of the Red Sea coast. But to make the Arab revolt really successful, Lawrence realised that they had to take the key port of Aqaba (see Source 2).

SOURCE 1
Lawrence of Arabia – the legend. Lawrence dressed in pure white silk with a head band of scarlet and gold, with a curved golden dagger at his waist. He dressed this way to impress the Arab tribes who lived in the desert (the Bedouin). Lawrence became famous for his toughness and courage

1. Why do you think the British encouraged the Arab revolt?
2. How did Lawrence become involved in the revolt?
3. Why did Lawrence dress like a rich and powerful Arab?

LAWRENCE OF ARABIA

In May 1917 Lawrence set out with a small force to undertake a 600-mile journey through a desert wasteland to sweep down on Aqaba. With him went Auda abu Tayi, a Bedouin chief who was the most famous warrior in Arabia and who had killed many Turks. Their journey became a legend of hardship and bravery as they raided Turkish bases. In one ferocious attack, Lawrence, leading the charge, accidentally shot his own camel. He nearly died as he fell to the ground and the other camels swept over him. Auda, meanwhile, danced around showing off six bullet holes in his robes.

Other Arabs joined them on the way so that it was a much larger force – around 1000 – that arrived outside the gates of Aqaba. Aqaba, weakened by lack of supplies, surrendered and on 6 July 1917 the Arab revolt marched triumphantly into the city.

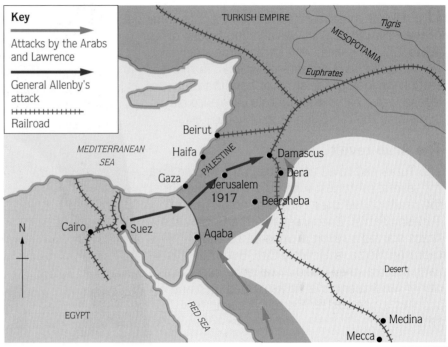

SOURCE 2 Map showing the major towns of the Arab campaign

Lawrence and Allenby

Lawrence himself travelled by camel across the Sinai Desert to tell the British that Aqaba had fallen. In Cairo, Lawrence met the new commander of the British forces, General Allenby.

Lawrence wanted the Arab revolt to be more than just a thorn in the side of the Turks; he wanted the Arabs to play a major role in winning the Middle Eastern campaign. He knew that Allenby and the Egyptian Expeditionary Force (EEF) were about to launch a major attack on Palestine. His plan was that the Arabs would attack the Turks from the rear. Allenby liked this idea and sent guns and supplies to Feisal.

Allenby did not want to get involved in the trench warfare he had seen on the Western Front. So he created gaps in the enemy lines and then sent his cavalry shooting through; they would then circle round and cut the enemy off. He pushed his troops to the limits of endurance to make the breakthroughs. It worked – by December 1917, the British had captured Jerusalem (see Source 2).

A new type of warfare

Lawrence became an expert in GUERRILLA WARFARE, raiding Turkish supply bases and blowing up bridges and railways. He used camels mounted with light machine guns to make daring attacks on the enemy. No one had used this form of fighting before. The Turks put a reward of £50,000 on his head.

He had a dedicated force of Arab bodyguards to protect him. In one attack on a Turkish troop train, seven lost their lives pulling Lawrence out of a hail of bullets. There was great competition to join the bodyguard because of Lawrence's reputation for endurance, adventure and hard fighting behind enemy lines.

Lawrence knew that image was important if he was to persuade other Arabs to join their forces. He shaved every day so that his red face and bright blue eyes would be immediately recognisable against his white robes. Lawrence and his fighters became a living legend amongst the desert Bedouin.

At the end of 1917 Lawrence went in disguise to Dera, a Turkish centre of communications, to spy out a way to attack the city. He was captured by the Turks although they did not realise who they had caught. He was tortured, beaten and sexually assaulted. Luckily, he managed to escape.

SOURCE 3 Lawrence on a camel in the desert. Lawrence carried an American Colt 'Wild West' revolver which he had taken from someone trying to kill him. This gun had been fired directly at him but the safety catch had been left on. Lawrence regarded it as a token of good luck. He also had a Lee Enfield rifle, given to him by Feisal, in which he carved notches for dead Turks until he grew tired of it, the number had grown so large

Exit Lawrence

In Damascus the arguments started about who should control the Middle East. When the news broke that the British and the French were to take control of large parts of the Middle East, the Arabs felt betrayed. They had expected to be rewarded for their part in the War. Lawrence, tired by the squabbling, and bitter about the treatment of the Arabs, left the Middle East.

Lawrence had played a crucial role in the Arab revolt and had been the vital link between the Arabs and the British forces. He developed tactics of guerrilla warfare, and with the Arabs, prevented thousands of Turkish troops from fighting against the main British force. As a leader, famed for his courage and endurance, he became a legend.

Some Arab historians, however, believe that his importance has been overrated by the British. They see him as a useful aid to their own leaders, who planned and directed the Arab revolt which pushed the Turks out of their homeland.

To Damascus

Throughout 1918 Allenby and the EEF moved up the left side of Palestine while the Northern Arab Army moved up the right. Lawrence and his forces continued their raids on the supply lines and Turkish outposts.

The Turks were pushed back. The fighting became cruel and bitter. In many Arab villages, it was discovered that the retreating Turks had raped and butchered women and children. After one such incident at the village of Taflas, Lawrence and the Arab forces, mad with anger, had charged a retreating Turkish column of 2000 and massacred them all.

Turks began to surrender in large numbers. In October 1918 the British and Arab armies met and triumphantly entered Damascus.

Activity

Explain how T.E. Lawrence became 'Lawrence of Arabia'. Show how he deliberately helped to create the legend and discuss his role in the Middle East campaign.

or

Do a storyboard for a film on Lawrence. Choose six episodes from his career and draw rough illustrations with notes explaining why these are significant. For example, you could start with one of Lawrence as a young officer and explain how he became involved in the Arab affairs, another might show him in Arab clothes and so on.

Why was the Eastern Front so important to the British and French?

IN AUGUST 1914 Tsar Nicholas II announced that Russia was entering the War against the Germans. Crowds in Petrograd, the Russian capital, cheered as the troops marched off to fight on the Eastern Front. Less than three years later, the Tsar was overthrown in the Russian Revolution of 1917 and the world's first COMMUNIST state was created. This event is so important in world history that it tends to overshadow Russia's contribution to the War. Some historians claim that the Russian army saved the British and French from defeat.

Evidence for this can be found at the very beginning of the War. The Germans had concentrated their forces in the west, in the plan to smash France. But two Russian forces attacked Germany on the Eastern Front and broke through their weak defences. This forced the Germans to transfer nine divisions to the east just as their thrust towards Paris reached its climax at the Battle of the Marne. The Germans lost the battle and any hope of a quick victory in the west.

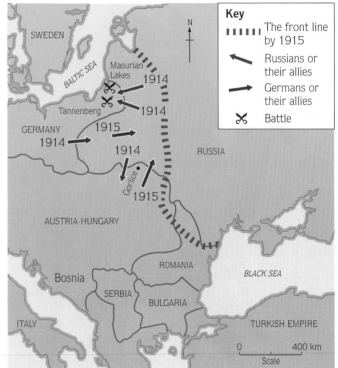

SOURCE 1 Map showing the Eastern Front

Early defeats

The Russians had not really been ready when they had been called upon to attack and they were hit hard when fresh German troops arrived on the Eastern Front. In 1914 they were defeated at the battles of Tannenberg and the Masurian Lakes, and almost 200,000 men were killed (see Source 3).

The reasons for these early defeats are not hard to find. The Russian generals were hopelessly incompetent and out of date. They believed that the 'Russian steamroller' would roll over its enemies by sheer weight of numbers. They did not take into account the power of the modern machine gun which the Germans had in large numbers.

The Russians were using maps which were 20 years old; their communications were extremely poor and they began to run short of weapons because their arms factories were not properly geared up for war. At times during the battles, they simply ran out of artillery shells and some guns were limited to firing three shells a day. Soldiers had to share one rifle between three men.

SOURCE 2 A train full of Russian prisoners, after the battle of Tannenberg

SOURCE 3 A description by a German officer of the slaughter at Tannenberg, quoted in *Britain at War*, Craig Mair, 1982.

66 *The sight of thousands of Russians driven into huge swamps or lakes to drown was ghastly . . . So fearful was the sight of these thousands of men with their guns, horses and ammunition, struggling in the water that, to shorten their agony, the Germans turned the machine guns on them. But even in spite of that, there was movement seen among them for a week after. And the mowing down of the cavalry brigade at the same time, 500 mounted men on white horses, all killed and packed so closely together that they remained standing.* 99

SOURCE 4 German cartoon of 1915, showing the Russian commander-in-chief, Grand Duke Nicholas, leaving the battlefield after another Russian defeat

1915 – Retreat

In May 1915 the Germans and Austrians launched a major offensive hoping to knock Russia out of the War. The Russians were in continual retreat for the rest of the year. Only the winter saved them from total defeat. However, the Russian army was not destroyed and thousands of German troops were tied down on the Eastern Front throughout 1915.

The retreat of 1915 allowed the Russians to recover. They were now nearer to their supply bases, whereas the Germans and Austrians were further away from theirs. Russian industry was turning out more weapons and the British and French were sending military equipment. By 1916 the Russian army was better equipped than at the start of the War.

1916 – Attack

In the spring of 1916 the French were in great trouble as the Germans mounted a determined assault on Verdun. The French sent urgent requests to the Russians to help by attacking in the east. The brilliant Russian commander, Brusilov, launched a huge offensive against the Austrians, driving them back and recapturing much of the territory lost in 1915. The Germans were forced to move 35 divisions from the Western Front to help the Austrians. Verdun was saved and the pressure on the French was relieved. But, as we shall see, Russia was to pay a high price for helping the French.

1. Make a list of things that were wrong with the Russian army at the beginning of the War.
2. What do you think the German cartoonist in Source 4 was trying to say:
a) about Russian commanders
b) about what the fighting was like?
3. Explain how crucial the fighting on the Eastern Front was to the British and French on the Western Front between 1914 and 1916? Use the table below to help you.

Year	Eastern Front	Western Front
1914	First Russian attack	Battle of the Marne
1915	Russian retreat	British and French relieved from German pressure
1916	Brusilov offensive	Verdun

SOURCE 5 Russian soldiers deserting in early 1917

SOURCE 6 From letters written by Russian soldiers, *The Russian Soldier's Morale from the Evidence of Tsarist Military Censorship*, Irina Davidian, 1996

Everybody is in low spirits. Soldiers have no more confidence in victory. And now there is the bad weather as well. We haven't received bread for two weeks. I am at my post all the time – frozen, soaked and, on top of that, hungry as a dog . . . Our position is bad, we're still retreating and the main reason is lack of shells . . . And it is the war ministers who did it. And now we have to use up the men instead of shells.

How did the Eastern Front collapse?

The winter of 1916 was a bad time for Russian soldiers and the Russian people.

The Russian army

The arrival of German troops after Brusilov's successful offensive in the summer saw the Russian army retreating again. Valuable weapons were lost and the army was soon short of ammunition and medical supplies. The winter of 1916 was particularly harsh and troops began to desert in increasing numbers. Sources 6 and 7 show how they felt.

However, events elsewhere in Russia were going to have a more dramatic effect on the Eastern Front.

The Russian people

Shortages of food and fuel meant that people were hungry and cold. The Russian railway system was breaking down under the strain placed on it by the War. Trains were being used to take troops and supplies to the warfront, so food was not getting to the cities. Added to this, much less food was being produced because peasants and horses were taken into the army, leaving fewer people to do all the work on the land.

SOURCE 7 From letters written by Russian soldiers, as in Source 7 above

All our divisions were defeated by the Germans. Perhaps, we'll have soon to admit that our war campaign is lost . . . The war has dragged on and one cannot see the end . . . This war is so hateful. The troops bear the brunt of everything, but now they don't want to attack . . . They say: 'Stop murdering people.'

1. Looking at Sources 5–7, how strong do you think the Russian army was at the beginning of 1917?
2. a) Why might this evidence be misleading about Russia's military strength?
   b) What does modern research say?
3. How was the War affecting people in the cities?

Revolution

The situation got worse in the Russian cities at the beginning of 1917. The Tsar had taken personal charge of the War in 1915, so he was blamed for the defeats. He had left his wife, the Tsarina, in charge of the government and she had made a terrible mess of running the country. People demanded a fundamental change in the way Russia was governed and in March 1917, the Tsar was forced to give up his throne.

A temporary 'Provisional Government' was set up to run Russia. It carried on with the War because it did not want Russia to be defeated by the Germans and wanted the future support of the British and French. But the Russian army and the Russian people had had enough. When a revolutionary leader called Lenin returned to Russia calling for peace, he gained a lot of support. In October 1917 Lenin and his party, the BOLSHEVIKS, seized power and formed the world's first communist government.

SOURCE 9 Lenin opposed the First World War: he claimed that millions of workers were being killed for no good reason. When unrest in Russia mounted in autumn 1917, Lenin was still in exile in Switzerland. The Germans helped him to travel back to Petrograd in the hope that he would cause trouble by speaking out against the War

The end of the Eastern Front

In March 1918 the new Bolshevik government made a peace treaty with Germany at Brest-Litovsk (see Source 8). The Bolsheviks had promised to end the War and had no choice but to agree to Germany's terms. The Germans gained a vast amount of valuable land and resources. They could also move thousands of troops back to the Western Front.

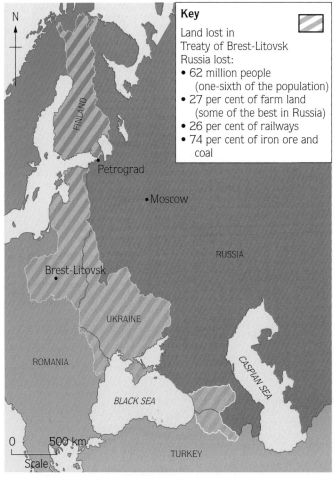

Key

Land lost in
Treaty of Brest-Litovsk
Russia lost:
- 62 million people
  (one-sixth of the population)
- 27 per cent of farm land
  (some of the best in Russia)
- 26 per cent of railways
- 74 per cent of iron ore and
  coal

SOURCE 8 The Treaty of Brest-Litovsk

Activity

It is March 1918. You are a journalist reporting on the collapse of the Eastern Front for a British newspaper. You have only 150 words to explain:
a) why the Eastern Front has collapsed. List the factors, but explain **why** each is important.
b) why this development is worrying to the British and French, but helpful to the Germans.

How did the War come to an end?

Germany's last chance

When the Eastern Front collapsed and the Russians stopped fighting, the Germans were able to transfer one million troops to France. The German army commanders knew that time was running out for them.

Two key factors meant that the Germans had to defeat the Allies quickly if they were to win at all.

The blockade

By 1918 the British naval blockade was biting hard. It is estimated that over a quarter of a million Germans died of starvation in 1917 and the numbers were even greater in 1918. There were strikes and demonstrations in northern cities as many civilians demanded an end to the War.

The arrival of American troops

In 1917 the Germans had used unrestricted submarine warfare to try to starve Britain out. This involved sinking American ships, which made it likely that the USA would enter the War. The Germans hoped they would win before American troops could make a difference. The USA declared war on Germany in April 1917 but it was over a year before it could get its troops properly trained and equipped. The first American troops reached the Western Front in May 1918.

The final stages

General Ludendorff was in charge of the last great offensive in March 1918, and he planned to break the stalemate. Instead of an 'over the top' frontal assault by a wave of troops, he sent small groups of 'stormtroopers' to attack all the way along the front line. It was a success – the Germans broke through the line and drove the Allies back more than 60 kilometres. Once again, as in 1914, the German army was in sight of Paris.

But by August 1918 the German army was exhausted and could not reach Paris. The Allies had fought hard to hold their positions and American troops were now joining them.

It was now the turn of the Allies to push forward and they were helped by new technology. Better tanks tore huge holes in the German defences. The Allies advanced more kilometres in a day than they had done in all the months of previous fighting. The Germans withdrew to the Hindenburg Line, a line of concrete bunkers and heavy defences. They could have made a strong stand here but other events were taking a hand.

SOURCE 1 Map of the last stages of the Western Front

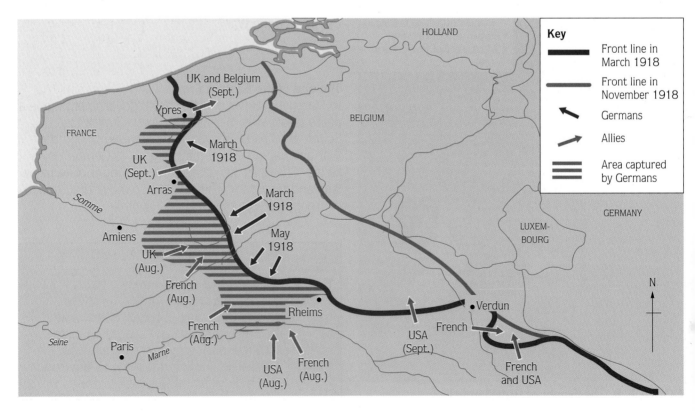

Armistice

By the beginning of November, all of Germany's allies – Austria, Turkey and Bulgaria – had surrendered. In the northern ports, German sailors mutinied and in Berlin crowds marched through the streets demanding an end to the War. There were food riots and strikes in other German cities. The Kaiser, unable to take the mounting pressure, fled to Holland.

A new German government was formed and immediately asked for a ceasefire.

SOURCE 2 A member of the German government in October 1918

We have no meat, potatoes cannot be delivered because we are short of 4000 trucks a day. Fat is unobtainable. The shortage is so great it is a mystery to me what the people of Berlin live on. The workers say 'Better a horrible end than an endless horror.'

SOURCE 3 Letter from General Hindenburg to German government, November 1918

The supreme commander demands an immediate dispatch of a peace offer to our enemies. There no longer exists any hope of forcing peace on our enemies. The enemy can bring in new and fresh reserves. The German army holds fast and repulses all attacks with success. But we must stop fighting to save the German people further useless sacrifices.

At the eleventh hour of the eleventh day of the eleventh month of 1918 an ARMISTICE was signed. All fighting stopped. The Germans had surrendered.

SOURCE 4 Sergeant Grady's diary, 11.11.1918

Machine gun company on my right lost 12 men at 10.55, when a high explosive landed in their position . . . At 11 o'clock sharp the shelling ceased on both sides.

1. Why did the Germans have one last chance to win the War at the beginning of 1918?
2. On your own copy of Source 1 add labels to describe the final stages of the War. Use the text on pages 82–83 to help you.
3. Why, according to Sources 2 and 3, did the Germans surrender?

Activity

1. The statements below give reasons why Germany lost the War. Which ones do you think are the most/least important?
a) First, write down the three reasons you think are the most important.
b) Then underneath, write the two you think are the next most important.
c) Lastly, write the three you think are least important at the bottom.
2. Then write a short essay: Why did Germany lose the War?
   Start with the most important reasons. You must explain each reason fully. For example, you should explain how America's entry into the War helped cause the German defeat.

The German navy failed to gain control of the seas.

The British naval blockade created shortages which brought Germany to the point of collapse.

The Russians on the Eastern Front saved the British and French from defeat.

America entered the War.

The German U-boat campaign failed.

Germany's allies were weak.

The German army was defeated.

British tank technology helped make the final breakthrough.

How was Britain organised to fight the War?

THE Great War was the first war to have a major impact on the lives of ordinary people back in Britain. In some ways everyone in Britain was 'fighting the War' and everyone's life was changed by it.

Hating the Germans

The first job of the government was to make sure that people in Britain stayed in favour of the War. One way of doing this was to whip up people's hatred of the Germans, so the government produced anti-German propaganda. Some of it was true. Much of it was not.

In 1915 the government published a report on German atrocities in Belgium during the first months of the War. The report quoted hundreds of 'eye-witness' reports of German cruelty. One person said he'd seen a soldier drive his BAYONET into a child's stomach, lift the child into the air on his bayonet, and carry it away while he and his comrades were singing. Another report told of a twelve-year-old boy whose hands had been cut off by the Germans because he clung to his parents who were being thrown on a fire.

Early in 1915 one of the most famous propaganda stories of all began to circulate – that there was a German factory where human corpses gathered from the battlefield were melted down so that the fat could be made into soap. In fact, captions to two separate photographs of dead horses and dead men had been swapped around.

SOURCE 1 From an advertisement for Black Cat cigarettes

SOURCE 2 From the magazine *John Bull*

" *If by chance you should discover one day in a restaurant that you are being served by a German waiter, you will throw the soup in his foul face.* "

The government's campaign of hatred against the Germans was very successful. German people living in Britain were attacked. In 1915 the government decided to hold prisoner all Germans between the ages of seventeen and 45. German old men, women and children were sent back to Germany.

By 1917 anti-German feeling was so strong that even the King decided that he had to change his family name from Saxe-Coburg-Gotha to Windsor!

Civilian casualties

In the early months of the War people feared that Britain would be invaded. On 17 December 1914 the British people read these headlines in their morning newspapers.

GERMANS CREEP OUT TO ATTACK EAST COAST . . . SCARBOROUGH, HARTLEPOOL AND WHITBY SHELLED FOR 30 MINUTES

In fact, 119 people, including babies and children, had been killed. Source 3 shows how this German attack was used as propaganda by the government.

50,000,000 CARTOONS WINNING THE WAR
Black Cat Cigarettes

Death drinks the toast of *Blood* — of slain soldiers and civilians, and of innocent women and children, killed wherever the German troops have over-run.

This grim picture shows the inevitable fate the Kaiser has prepared for himself and Germany. War and Hunger are leading him by the hand — *to the end*.

The *biting truth* of these extraordinary cartoons — there are 140 different ones in colour — completely and finally proves WHY we are at war with Germany. And that is why every packet of BLACK CAT cigarettes (4d., 3½d., or 3d.) contains one of the *50,000,000* of these cartoons, fifty million *truths* to combat German *lies*.

SOURCE 3 A poster issued by the government soon after the attack on Scarborough

SOURCE 5 The scene after the Silvertown Disaster, 1917

1. Why do you think the Germans bombed the east coast towns?
2. How might it have helped their war effort?
3. How do you think the inhabitants responded to this attack?

In 1915 the Germans started to send great airships called Zeppelins on bombing raids to Britain. These were almost 200 metres long and could drop up to 27 tonnes of bombs. East Anglia, London and towns in the south-east were the main targets. Hundreds of people were killed.

SOURCE 4 An eye-witness account of a Zeppelin Raid in 1915

The whole street seemed to explode. There was smoke and flames all over, but the worst of it was the screams of the dying and the wounded and mothers looking frantically for their kids.

Another serious incident took place on 19 January 1917 at Silvertown in East London. A MUNITIONS factory went up in flames and exploded, killing 69 people and injuring 400. Factories and nearby houses were blown to bits.

SOURCE 6 An eye-witness account by Mabel Bastable, who was a schoolgirl in 1917

There were shouts of 'Fire!', well, you couldn't miss it, the whole place was lit up. We were all outside looking . . .

I went upstairs to get a shawl. Suddenly, I was downstairs and the house was on top of me. It's funny but I can't really remember hearing the explosion . . . Our house was blown down right enough.

We had to walk a long way to find somewhere to put up [sleep], my Mum's sister I think we stayed with. We didn't go up to Silvertown again . . . I didn't go to school again. There was no school, no house, so there was no point.

A total of 1500 British civilians were killed during the War. That might seem low to us by the standards of more recent wars, but at that time it was very high compared to previous wars.

Activity

Write a propaganda report on the explosion at Silvertown using the evidence in Sources 5 and 6. You should slant your report to whip up hatred of the German enemy. Remember that this is the result of an accident and not of bombing, but if you are clever you can still use it as propaganda.

DORA

People's lives were also greatly affected by the passing of the Defence of the Realm Act, or DORA. This listed all the things people were no longer allowed to do now that Britain was at war, and also gave the government special powers. The first measures were introduced on 8 August 1914. During the War other rules were added.

Under DORA the people of Britain were not allowed to:

- talk about naval or military matters in public places
- spread rumours about military affairs
- trespass on railways or bridges
- fly a kite
- light bonfires or fireworks
- buy binoculars
- trespass on allotments
- melt down gold or silver
- give bread to dogs, chickens or horses
- use invisible ink when writing abroad
- buy whisky or brandy in a railway refreshment room or similar place
- ring church bells.

The government of Britain could:

- try any civilian breaking these laws
- take possession of any factory or workshop
- take any land it needed
- censor newspapers.

As the War continued, the government brought in many other measures. For example:

- it introduced British Summer Time (putting the clocks forward an hour) to give more daylight for work in the evening
- it cut down on pub opening hours
- it gave instructions for beer to be watered down
- customers in pubs were not allowed to buy rounds of drinks.

---

1. Write the heading DORA in your book and then make two lists – one headed 'Sensible Ideas' and the other 'Stupid Ideas'. Put each of the measures described above into one of the lists.
2. Can you think of reasons for any of the laws in your second list?
3. Which of these measures do you think would be popular and which would be unpopular?

Feeding the realm

One of the aims of DORA was to prevent food shortages. At first, food shortage problems were caused by the British people themselves. As soon as war broke out they panicked and bought large amounts of food which they hoarded at home. Shops sold out completely within a few days. However, everybody gradually calmed down and shortages did not really become serious until the end of 1916.

Until that time much of Britain's food was still imported. But by 1917 the Germans were using their submarines to stop supply ships from getting through. In April 1917 Britain had only six weeks' worth of wheat stores! Food prices rose sharply and queues for food grew. It was a bleak year for most people. Coal was so short that in October it was RATIONED according to the number of rooms in the house.

In 1917 it was clear that the DORA measures were not enough to reduce the amount of food being eaten or increase the amount being produced. The government tried to operate a voluntary ration scheme. It asked people to limit themselves to four pounds of bread (1.80 kilograms), two and a half pounds of meat (1.13 kilograms) and three quarters of a pound of sugar (340 grams) each week. The King and Queen limited themselves to this ration and if you followed their example you were issued with a blue ribbon!

But the campaign failed – shortages of bread and potatoes continued. Many working people could not afford to buy meat and sugar anyway – their diet had consisted mainly of bread even before the rationing was introduced! The rich, on the other hand, continued to live as luxuriously as ever. Food was available for those who could afford it – on the BLACK MARKET if necessary.

Desperate attempts were made to grow more food. Nearly everybody started to keep an allotment where they could grow food. They turned parks and tennis courts into vegetable plots where they grew potatoes, turnips and carrots and kept chickens.

Under DORA the government had powers to take over land for growing food. In 1917 it decided to plough up an extra two and half million acres of land. The amount of land used for farming increased from eleven million acres in 1914 to fourteen million in 1918. However, many farm workers had joined the army, and so much of the work on this extra land was carried out by the new Women's Land Army. Prisoners of war and conscientious objectors (men who refused to join the army: see page 90) were used as well.

SOURCE 7 A 'Land Girl' painted by Cecil Aldin

When women were asked to sign up for the Women's Land Army 30,000 responded immediately. They did work that would have been done mainly by men before the War, and were paid the same wages as men. The work was hard – stone-picking, weeding, pulling turnips and haymaking. It made sense for the women to dress like men, but this made many people uneasy. As Source 8 shows, the government was keen for the women still to behave as people at the time thought women should.

SOURCE 8 Instructions to the members of the Women's Land Army

You are doing a man's work and so you are dressed rather like a man; but remember that . . . because you wear a smock and trousers you should take care to behave like an English girl who expects chivalry and respect from every one she meets. Noisy or ugly behaviour brings discredit, not only on yourself but upon the uniform, and the whole Women's Land Army. When people see you pass show them that an English girl who is working for her Country on the land is the best sort of girl.

Despite all these measures, by 1918 the situation was getting worse for most people. Food queues grew even longer. Signs of malnutrition were beginning to appear among the poorest people. The rich, on the other hand, still had plenty to eat. Resentment of the rich was growing fast. So to share the food round more fairly the government introduced compulsory rationing. Sugar was rationed from January 1918, and from April so were meat, butter, cheese and margarine. Everybody was issued with a ration card, and registered with a local butcher and grocer. Every person could have fifteen ounces of meat (425 grams), five ounces of bacon (142 grams) and four ounces of butter (113 grams) or margarine per week.

SOURCE 9 Evidence of food shortages

Rationing worked. Queueing for food soon became a thing of the past. And historians agree that by the time rationing ended the health of the poorest people in Britain was actually better than it had been in peacetime – partly because rationing meant they got a better share of healthy food.

SOURCE 10 From a government leaflet published during the War. A crust of bread is speaking

I am a slice of bread. I am wasted once a day by 48,000,000 people of Britain. I am 'the bit left over'; the slice eaten absent-mindedly when really I wasn't needed. I am the waste crust.
If you collected me and my companions for a whole week you would find that we amounted to 9380 tons [9530 tonnes] of good bread.
WASTED! Nine shiploads of good bread!
SAVE ME, AND I WILL SAVE YOU!

1. Look back at the list of 'stupid ideas' you made for question 1 on page 86. Does the evidence on the rest of this page help you to explain why these ideas were introduced?
2. Draw a timeline for the period August 1914 to April 1918. Mark on it the different methods used to feed Britain. Which one of these measures was the most important?

How did the factories keep going?

When war broke out industries such as textiles and dressmaking, which employed a lot of women, suffered because people no longer wanted to buy so many clothes. Many women lost their jobs. However, as more and more men went off to fight, somebody had to replace them in the factories and on the farms. Gradually, women began to take on men's jobs. But this did not happen overnight.

In 1915 the government was faced with a serious shortage of shells and bullets. Many more workers were needed, but of course the men were joining the army. Instead, the government would have to recruit as many women to work in factories as possible. A march to publicise the campaign to recruit women was organised by David Lloyd George, who was minister in charge of munitions, and Mrs Pankhurst, the Suffragette leader. This was the first time the government had accepted that women could play a vital role in winning the War.

The government drew up a register of women who were available for work. Over 100,000 registered, but only 5000 of them were given jobs, mainly because employers and male workers were prejudiced against having women working in industry.

The trade unions as well were very suspicious of women coming into factories and doing men's jobs. They were worried that women would work for lower wages and so the men would lose their jobs for good. However, in 1915 the government and the unions came to an agreement. Women workers were to be paid the same as men, but women would only be allowed to take over men's jobs 'for the duration of the War, or till sufficient male labour should again be available'.

Later in 1915 the army was so short of munitions that the government set up its own munitions factories, where there were no male employers or workers to stop women being employed.

> **1.** Was the campaign to recruit women workers successful? Explain your answer.

A turning point came when CONSCRIPTION was introduced in 1916. At this point many factory owners finally realised that they needed to take on women to replace the male workers who had joined the army.

Before the War it had been assumed that women could only do light, indoor work which did not need much strength or skill. This was why so many women worked as domestic servants. These views were soon shown to be wrong. During the War women learned new skills within a much shorter time than the normal training period. In many jobs women performed better than the men they were replacing, even though the conditions they worked in were often tougher than they had been for men before the War.

SOURCE 12
A munitions factory painted by E.F. Skinner

SOURCE 13
A fitter at the London Bus Company in 1918

SOURCE 11 A government report written after the War describing the situation in 1915

> *In every industrial district without exception, there was opposition to the introduction of women. In some cases this opposition led to strikes, in other cases it took the form of refusal to work with or train women, or attempts to discredit their efforts.*

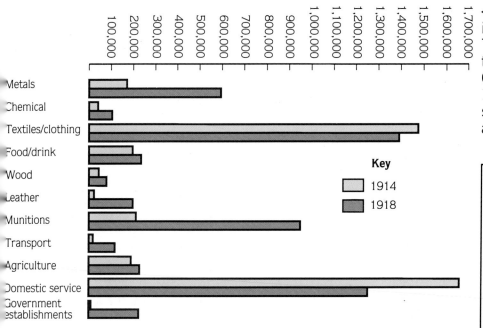

Metals
Chemical
Textiles/clothing
Food/drink
Wood
Leather
Munitions
Transport
Agriculture
Domestic service
Government establishments

100,000 200,000 300,000 400,000 500,000 600,000 700,000 800,000 900,000 1,000,000 1,100,000 1,200,000 1,300,000 1,400,000 1,500,000 1,600,000 1,700,000

Key
☐ 1914
■ 1918

◀**SOURCE 16** Women employed in industry in 1914 and 1918. These figures come mainly from the Report of the War Cabinet Committee on Women in Industry, 1919. The figures for domestic service, agriculture and transport are author's estimates

2. Look at the figures in Source 16 carefully. Find two industries where the number of women workers actually went down during the War. Why was this?
3. Some of the biggest increases were in metal industries, government establishments and agriculture. Why was this?
4. 'The War didn't lead to more women going out to work, but it changed the types of jobs women did.'
   Say whether you agree or disagree with this statement and why.
5. Do you think that by 1918 most men had accepted women as being equal to them?

SOURCE 14 Women workers at a Lancashire colliery in September 1918. The total workforce at this colliery was 9000, of whom 500 were women. They did not work underground, but did surface work such as sorting or carrying coal

SOURCE 15 Tar sprayers resurfacing a road in London

You have seen the ways in which people's lives were completely changed by the War. Working in pairs discuss the following questions:
1. Which of these changes do you think made British society better and fairer?
2. Which changes took their freedom away from people?
3. Which changes would you have kept once the War had ended?
4. Which changes do you think were actually kept after the War had ended?

Did anyone object to the War?

WHEN Britain declared war on Germany in 1914, the vast majority of British people supported the War. The government put out lots of propaganda to make sure people continued to support it. The newspapers – which were the main source of information for most people – were in favour of the War in any case. The Defence of the Realm Act made it difficult for people to criticise the way the War was being fought without getting into trouble. Only a few people publicly criticised the War. However, as the War progressed this situation began to change.

The conchies

From 1914 until 1916 the government relied on volunteers to fight in the army. But the huge numbers of casualties in France meant the government needed more and more soldiers. By 1916 it was clear that volunteers were not enough.

Many people in Britain were also angry to see some young men still enjoying themselves at home while others were risking their lives for their country. Pressure grew on the government to force all men to join up and fight. So in January 1916 the government brought in the Military Service Act, which introduced conscription for all single men between the ages of eighteen and 41. A second Act was passed in March 1916 to include married men.

Men who wanted to be exempt (excused) from military service had to appear before a military tribunal to present their case for being excused. The military tribunal included people from the army and a 'jury' made up of local people. Conscripts could be exempted if:

■ they proved they were not physically fit to serve *or*
■ they proved their job was essential to the war effort *or*
■ they proved they had genuine reasons of conscience for not wanting to fight. These men were known as 'conscientious objectors' or 'conchies'.

If the military tribunal thought their reasons were good enough they could get a Certificate of Exemption.

Roughly 16,000 men refused to join the army because they were conscientious objectors. Some of them believed that war itself was wrong and did not want to support it in any way. Others did not want to kill fellow human beings, but would help the War in other ways.

Here are some case studies gathered by the No-Conscription Fellowship, which supported conchies. They were published in 1919.

Case study 1: Stephen Hobhouse

Stephen Hobhouse is 36, married and a Quaker [Quakers believe in complete non-violence].

Despite his wealthy background, he has spent much of his adult life doing social work among the poor of the East End of London. He has for many years been opposed to war and military service because of deeply held religious views.

There can be no doubt as to his courage and to his willingness to face any danger or trouble for the sake of his religion. He spent some time in Turkey working with the poor and homeless.

He is undoubtedly physically unfit for active service and would be useless to the army. He has heart and stomach trouble and is extremely short-sighted.

His three brothers are in the army and his family are strongly in favour of the War, but they believe that he should be allowed to continue his work in the service of his God and his country.

He is now serving a sentence of two years. He has already served one sentence of 112 days' hard labour.

He says 'Four months in a prison cell have only confirmed my belief that war and violence are not the ways to overcome evil . . .'

Case study 2: G.H. Stuart Beavis

Beavis was 34 when the War broke out. He has lived in Germany and France and speaks both languages. He was a teacher of languages at a Working Men's College in London.

It was his great belief in the brotherhood of all nations which caused him to refuse conscription. In May 1916 he was taken to France. He was told that he was now in the war zone and liable to be shot for refusing to obey orders. He was tried and sentenced to death! This was later changed to ten years in prison.

Case study 3: Clifford Allen

Clifford Allen was 25 in 1914. He was well educated and had become a journalist. He was one of the founders of the No-Conscription Fellowship in November 1914 and was its first chairman. From 1916 onwards, he received a string of prison sentences with hard labour for refusing to join up. He gave the following reasons at his trial:

'I believe that you sitting here and the people of all nations on both sides want peace. I believe that it is the fault of the governments that this has not happened. I will not take part in any war which I believe could be stopped immediately. I resist war because I love freedom. Conscription is the denial of freedom. You can shut me up in prison over and over again, but you cannot imprison my free spirit.'

1. Stephen Hobhouse could have been excused from military service on grounds of ill health or because he was doing work 'of national importance', yet he chose not to. Why do you think this was?
2. Why did Stuart Beavis object to the War?

Activity

Clifford Allen is critical of governments. He thinks the War could be stopped right away. He believes that war itself is wrong. He is opposed to conscription because it takes away the freedom of individuals. He is prepared to go to prison for his beliefs.

In pairs, act out a conversation between Clifford Allen and a member of a military tribunal who is trying to convince him that he should play an active part in the War.

SOURCE 1 This cartoon was published in a PACIFIST newspaper called the *Workers' Dreadnought* in 1916

What did people think of the conchies?

As you can imagine, a lot of pressure was put on the conchies. They were given some support by certain magazines (see Source 1) and by organisations such as the No-Conscription Fellowship, a group of conscientious objectors. But they were treated as if they were cowards, traitors or criminals by the army, by the government, and even by many ordinary people in Britain. White feathers (a symbol of cowardice) were handed out to young men who had not joined the army, regardless of any reasons they might have had for not fighting.

Even those who agreed to do war work other than fighting were outcasts. The government found it impossible to get employers to take on conchies in their factories. It ended up setting up its own work camps where conchies had to do work such as quarrying and crushing stone or repairing roads.

1. Write a sentence summarising the message of each of the cartoons in Sources 1 and 2.
2. Which side would you take?

SOURCE 2 This cartoon was published in *John Bull* magazine, May 1918. The caption read 'This little pig stayed at home'

DID ANYONE OBJECT TO THE WAR?

Sources 3–5 show the range of attitudes at the time.

SOURCE 3 Comments made by members of military tribunals to conchies

66■ *It is such people as you who cause wars . . .*
■ *You are only fit to be on the end of a German bayonet . . .*
■ *You are nothing but a shivering mass of unwholesome fat . . .*
■ *A man who would not help to defend his own country is a coward . . .*99

SOURCE 4 From a speech by the government minister Lord Derby in the House of Lords on 24 May 1917

66*They are prepared to let other men in this country fight for their freedom, but they will not even assist their country by doing any work at all for the nation.*99

SOURCE 5 From a report by a Quaker conchy, quoted in *The Modern World* by Tim Wood and Chris Jordan, published in 1989

66*It was right at the beginning that I learnt that the only people from whom I could expect sympathy were soldiers and not the civilians.*

I was waiting in the guardroom when five soldiers under arrest came in. When they asked me what I was in for, I was as simple as possible. 'I am a Quaker and I refused to join the army because I think that war is murder.'

'Murder,' one of them whispered. 'It's bloody murder.'

*As they went away they each came up to me and shook me by the hand – 'Stick to it matey,' they said, one after the other.*99

1. What do you think the speaker meant by the first comment in Source 3?
2. Which of the sources above suggest that the conchies were cowards and traitors?
3. Do you think these were fair comments?

What happened to the conchies?

Most conchies joined up to do war work in the medical services or support services. For example, they became stretcher bearers and played as brave a part as anyone in the fight against the Germans on the Western Front.

Only about 1500 conchies refused every kind of alternative service. They went to prison until the end of the War. Ten died in prison, another 63 died soon after release, and 31 of them went mad as a result of their experiences.

SOURCE 6 An account of the treatment of conscientious objectors in a military prison in England, written in 1928

66*At Cleethorpes, a War Resister called James Brightmore was put in a pit three feet by two feet and twelve feet deep with two feet of water in the bottom. He was kept there for four days. He was told by an officer that five of his companions had been sent to France and shot, and that he would be the next to go.*

*Another man called Jack Gray was put into a sack, thrown into a pond eight times and pulled out by a rope around his body.*99

SOURCE 7 While in military prisons in France, several conchies were given severe punishments, including 'crucifixion', which meant being tied to a gun carriage for hours. A description written in 1928

66*. . . Our ankles were tied together and our arms then tied tightly at the wrists to the cross and we had to remain in that position for two hours.*

*The second evening we were placed with our faces to the barbed wire of a fence . . . I found myself drawn so closely to the fence that when I wished to turn my head I had to do so very carefully to avoid my face being torn. To make matters worse, it came on to rain and a bitterly cold wind blew across the top of the hill.*99

1. Do you think the conscientious objectors were cowards or very brave men? Use Sources 1–7 to support your answer.

One man's experience: Siegfried Sassoon

Most of the people we have studied in this section were not famous. Their opposition to the War was only known to the few people closest to them. There were others, however, whose opposition was more public. We are going to look at the views of one famous person, the poet Siegfried Sassoon, and see how his views changed during the War.

Siegfried Sassoon was born in 1886. He was a writer and a poet. He came from a very comfortable background in the south of England. Apart from writing, he spent much of his time fox-hunting or playing cricket and golf.

He joined the army in July 1914, before war broke out. He fought bravely on the Western Front, won the Military Cross (a medal for bravery) for a single-handed attack on a trench, and was recommended for a Victoria Cross. He was wounded in 1916 during the Battle of the Somme. Back home in Britain his war poetry quickly made him famous (see Source 6 on page 36).

Sassoon's poems contained many attacks on people who were not directly involved in the fighting yet who supported the War – the old men, the generals, the journalists, the civilians (see Source 9).

Sassoon returned to France to fight, but he became totally opposed to the War. He was not a conscientious objector, but he hated the War because he thought it was unnecessary. He also hated the attitude of the people at home, because he thought they had no idea what life in the trenches was really like. But he still continued to fight. In July 1917 he was wounded again.

Back in England, encouraged by friends who were against the War, he made the statement in Source 10 to his commanding officer.

SOURCE 8 Written by Sassoon years after the War about his decision to join the army in July 1914

66*I rushed to the conclusion that war was a certainty, so what else could I do but try to have a gun in my hands when the Germans arrived, even if I did not know how to fire it properly? . . . I said to myself that I was ready to meet whatever the War might ask of me. After all, dying for one's native land was believed to be the most glorious thing one could possibly do.*99

SOURCE 9 *The General,* a poem written in 1917

66*'Good morning; good morning!' the general said
When we met him last week on our way to the line.
Now the soldiers he smiled at are most of 'em dead.
And we're cursing his staff for incompetent swine.
'He's a cheery old card,' grunted Harry to Jack
As they slogged up to Arras with rifle and pack.
But he did for them both with his plan of attack.*99

SOURCE 10 Sassoon's statement

66*A Soldier's Declaration*
*I believe the War is being prolonged by those who have the power to end it. I believe that this war upon which I entered as a war of defence and liberation has now become a war of conquest and aggression. I have seen and endured the sufferings of the troops and I can no longer be a party to prolong these sufferings for ends which I believe to be evil and unjust.*99

The statement was printed in the *Bradford Pioneer* on 27 July 1917. Three days later it was read out in the House of Commons, and the next day it was printed in the *Daily Mail* and *The Times.*

He expected to be COURT MARTIALLED, but instead he was sent for psychiatric treatment in a hospital specialising in victims of shell-shock. In 1918 he returned once again to fight in France, where he was again wounded.

After the War, Sassoon became a pacifist. In 1919 he announced, 'I have pledged myself to oppose war in every way I can.'

---

1. How did Sassoon's view of the War change between 1914 and 1919?
2. Look at Source 8. Why did Sassoon join the army in the first place?
3. Sources 9 and 10 give similar reasons for Sassoon's opposition to the War. What are they?
4. Which of Sources 9 and 10 do you think expresses his views more clearly?

What kind of country did the soldiers come back to?

Armistice Day

The armistice, signed on 11 November 1918, brought all fighting to an end. Germany surrendered. The bloodiest war the world had ever known left almost nine million dead, of whom nearly a million were from Britain and its Empire.

News of the armistice brought crowds out onto the streets of London. People danced in Trafalgar Square and flocked to Buckingham Palace. The ringing of bells, and people singing and cheering echoed throughout the capital. In cities and towns throughout Britain, marching bands were hastily organised.

In some places, including the warfront in France, the celebrations were quieter, mixed with relief and sorrow for those who had been killed. But everybody was glad it was over. The soldiers looked forward to going home and the people in Britain looked forward to the heroes' return.

The heroes' return

Only a few weeks after the armistice, on 14 December 1918, there was a General Election. The new COALITION government, including Liberal and Conservative MPs, announced that its aims were: 'To make Britain a fit country for heroes to live in' and to 'get back to normal'.

SOURCE 1 Front page of the *Daily Mirror*, 12 November 1918

YESTERDAY-THE TRENCHES

TO-DAY-UNEMPLOYED

SOURCE 2
Posters published
by the Labour Party

The government had planned to release men from the army slowly, over a number of years, but many soldiers wanted to get home to their families straight away. Over two million men, some of them healthy, some disabled and wounded, returned from the trenches. For many of them the problems started immediately, as you can see in Sources 2–5.

SOURCE 3 Written by the novelist Barbara Cartland in 1978

In the country, chicken farms, wayside cafes and garages have sprung up like mushrooms – all run by ex-servicemen. Many of these have already gone bankrupt and their owners have joined the patient queues of hollow-eyed men . . . waiting for a job.

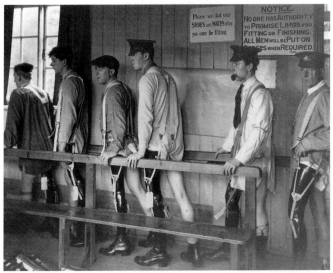

SOURCE 4 Soldiers being fitted with artificial legs. By 1920 more than 40,000 men were fitted with artificial limbs

SOURCE 5 An account by Grace Hayward, who lived in Ore, a small village near Hastings, during the War

After the dreadful First War, they came up and used to stand outside our gate and sing. They were so poverty struck, those that had gone and fought for us . . .
They'd lost arms, been blinded. They were begging, selling matches. They used to stand about playing an old accordion, standing on one leg. Those poor men.

For the returning heroes there was only limited unemployment benefit, and there was no National Health Service. Housing for many was cramped, unhealthy or non-existent. Many unemployed or wounded soldiers relied on their families or on charity to look after them. Many of the disabled did not qualify for an army pension. To make matters worse, between 1918 and 1920 a terrible flu epidemic hit Britain. Thousands of people died in Britain, and twenty million died around the world – more people than died in the War itself.

The new government passed various reforms between 1918 and 1920:

■ **1918** The Education Act raised the school leaving age to fourteen.
■ **1919** The Ministry of Health Act set up a government department to check living conditions and to introduce measures to fight illness.
■ **1919** The Housing Act ordered local authorities to provide houses for 'the heroes'.
■ **1920** The Unemployment Insurance Act extended the 1911 Act (see page 4) to anyone earning less than £250 a year.

---

4. What are the people in Source 2 complaining about?
5. What reasons can you find for the fact that some ex-soldiers had to turn to begging to survive?
6. Which of the government's reforms would have been of most use to the soldiers in Sources 2–5?
7. Which of the reforms were brought in as a result of the War?
8. Do you think the government was succeeding in creating a country fit for heroes to live in?

'Homes fit for heroes'

This was the slogan of the government's housing campaign. Even before the War Britain had been short of houses. To make matters worse, during the War many houses had not been well looked after and had become unfit to live in. When millions of soldiers suddenly arrived back in England the problem became severe. Many of them could not rely on relatives or friends to house them or their families.

The Housing Act of 1919 meant that local councils had to provide homes for the working classes in their areas. Over 200,000 new houses were built in the next three years. Even so, this was nowhere near enough for all the soldiers and their families, because the birth rate increased enormously after the War.

While soldiers were waiting for new council houses they had to live in temporary accommodation, some of which was very bad. In Brighton and Hove on the south coast of England, for example, some soldiers and their families were housed in old slums to start with.

> **1.** Look at Source 6. St Helens Council did a good job. But what problem did it not solve?

> **SOURCE 6** A report from St Helens in Lancashire in the early 1920s
>
> *The Council was very good – it built very good houses. The standard was very high. They had some first class supervisory staff. The Clerk of the Works, who had been a builder himself, was on the job all day long. The queues for the houses were miles long. Everyone put their names on the list. They jumped for joy if they got a council house.*

SOURCE 7 Lynton Mews, Bermondsey, London, in 1919

> **2.** Study Source 8. Working with a partner make a list of all the ways in which the new home is better than the old one.
> **3.** Are there any ways in which it is worse?

SOURCE 8 An artist's reconstruction of a house in Hereford Street, Brighton. The old house was demolished in 1925 and the new council house was built in its place

New products

Sources 9–13 show adverts for new products which first became available soon after the War. Some of them had been developed or made cheaper as a direct result of the War. These new products changed the lives of people who could afford them, often for the better.

▼**SOURCE 9** An advert for electric lights

B.S.A MOTOR BICYCLES

XCEL
ALL BRITISH
ELECTRIC DOMESTIC APPLIANCES

Wonderland!

OSRAM LAMPS

THE LIGHT FOR ALL

WONDERFUL!–20 HOURS FOR ONE PENNY!

▲**SOURCE 11** An advert for motorcycles

▲**SOURCE 12** A 1920s advert for domestic appliances

For Unoccupied Evenings

Bachelor quarters may be the snuggest in the world, but nowhere else on the long winter evenings is one so often at a loose end.

Install a Marconiphone Wireless Receiver, and you will never be at a loss for entertainment. The British Broadcasting Company take the solution of the problem out of your hands. Their admirably varied programmes are yours whenever you care to "tune in."

The Marconiphone is the Receiver on which you can always rely, for in it is summed up everything for which the name "Marconi" stands in Wireless.

The best Christmas present—for your family or your friends—is

Admirably adapted for general purposes throughout Great Britain, the **MARCONIPHONE V2** is a two-valve receiver of extreme sensitiveness and perfect workmanship. Price complete with head-phones, valves, batteries, etc., including B.B.C. Tariff 15/-.

£19 : 4 : 6

The **Marconiphone**

The Triumph of the Master Mind

MARCONI'S WIRELESS TELEGRAPH CO. LTD., MARCONI HOUSE, STRAND, W.C.:
Principality Buildings, Queen Street, CARDIFF; 101 St. Vincent Street, GLASGOW; 10 Cumberland Street, Deansgate, MANCHESTER; 38 Northumberland Street, NEWCASTLE-ON-TYNE.

▼**SOURCE 10** An advert for Austin cars, 1926

£295

The tremendous and ever-growing popularity of the Austin Twelve, and the arrangements we have made for vastly increased production, have enabled us to reduce the prices of all models very substantially indeed, so that they now range in price from £295 to £425 at Works. If you have denied yourself the joys of Austin ownership on the score of price, that bar to full motoring enjoyment is now entirely removed. The "Clifton" Tourer at £295 is undoubtedly the finest value in the motoring world to-day. In initial cost it compares favourably with any; in serviceable quality it far surpasses most.

SOURCE 13 An advert for a radio set. The BBC was set up in 1922, when 125,000 radio licences were issued

The **Austin Twelve**

NEW REDUCED PRICES.......£295 to £425
AUSTIN TWENTY MODELS FROM....£475 to £715
AUSTIN SEVEN.....................£149

Send for full Catalogue.

The AUSTIN MOTOR CO., Ltd., Longbridge, BIRMINGHAM.
LONDON: Showrooms, Service Depot & Hire Dept.: 479-483, OXFORD STREET, W 1 (near Marble Arch).

1. Can you work out what each of the numbered items in Source 12 would be used for?
2. If you were rich and had the money to afford all the items in Sources 9–13, in which order would you buy them? List them in order.
3. If you were poor and lived in the council house in Source 8, earning £3 per week and paying a rent of ten shillings (50p) per week, which items do you think you could afford?
4. Were any of these inventions useful in any way during the War on the Western Front?
5. Most of these items were not available before the War. Why do you think they appeared for sale shortly after the War ended?

Getting back to normal

In 1918 the government said that one of its aims was to get the country 'back to normal' – which for most people meant getting back to how things were before the War.

Most restrictions imposed under DORA (see page 86) were ended. Food rationing, for example, was gradually phased out: meat rationing ended in November 1919, butter rationing early in 1920 and sugar rationing in November 1920.

But other things could not be normalised so easily.

Industry – back to normal?

As you saw on page 9, before the War there were many strikes and industrial disputes. When the War broke out these were shelved. At first it was considered unpatriotic to complain about working conditions. Employers no longer kept to some of the existing laws which had protected workers against long hours and poor conditions. Shift work, Sunday work, short meal times and longer working days all became normal. Many of the women working in factories did so under much tougher conditions than men had had to put up with before the War. The government had enormous powers. Strikes were made illegal and in some industries the government even fixed the wages.

In 1916, when conscription was introduced, employers gained even more power over their workers because they were able to influence whether or not a worker was conscripted. An employer could prevent a skilled worker being called up if he said the worker was important. Some workers were afraid that if they asked for higher wages they would be sent to the trenches.

The government could not have produced all the weapons and food it needed during the War without the hard work and co-operation of the unions and the workers. And for much of the War the nation was united in supporting the changes in industry. But gradually unrest began to spread among the workers.

By 1917 food prices were twice what they had been in 1914. Workers demanded higher wages – particularly the railwaymen and the miners. In 1917 strikes started. There was even some talk of contacting German and Russian and French workers and agreeing not to fight any more. In Britain this was seen as treason.

After the War it was soon clear that industrial unrest had returned. The miners, railwaymen, cotton spinners and even the London police went on strike in 1918. In 1919 the railwaymen went on strike again, while the armed forces formed a union to try to get increased pay, shorter hours of duty and decent pensions. They also wanted a promise from the government that they would not be used as strike breakers. This really worried the government.

The War was followed by a trade slump around the world. By 1921 two million people in Britain were unemployed and employers began to reduce wages. This was the start of trouble in the coal industry that eventually led to the General Strike in 1926.

Meanwhile, the Labour Party, representing the growing trade union movement, had more MPs than ever before and was becoming a political force to be reckoned with.

SOURCE 14 Striking miners. A photograph taken in 1921

---

1. Look back at page 9. Would you say that problems in industry after the War were more or less serious than the problems before the War?
2. Did the War make the position of the unions in Britain stronger or weaker?
   Give reasons for both your answers.

Attitudes – back to normal?

Some historians say that the War brought about changes in people's attitudes which made it almost impossible to turn the clock back. The War had caused great divisions between the generations. Young people were no longer so willing to follow the advice or ideas of the older generation. The War had made many young people independent, whether they were teenage soldiers thrown into the conflict in France or women who had volunteered to work on the land or in the nursing services. They did not intend to give up this independence as soon as the War was over.

Many leading writers and artists were angry with the way the 'old men' had run the War. They were angry with the way the newspapers had hidden the truth about the War from the ordinary people. Very soon hard-hitting books and poems about the War began to appear.

But there were many people who simply wanted to forget the sadness and tragedy of the war years – even those who had lost members of their family in the fighting, or who had been injured themselves. They also wanted to forget the shortages and the restrictions of the war years. They wanted to enjoy themselves.

SOURCE 17 A cartoon of a 'flapper', drawn in 1925. A 'flapper' was a young woman who wore short skirts, cut her hair short, wore lots of make-up, smoked cigarettes and drank cocktails. These things may seem normal now, but it appeared very daring at the time and would have been disapproved of by many older people

SOURCE 15 Written by a Wiltshire farmer, A.G. Street, about the years 1918–21

... We all had money to burn. I find this hard to write. It is not a pleasant thing to set down on paper what a tawdry life one lived in those few years ... But the majority of farmers took no thought for tomorrow, their only idea was to have a good time. Instead of living for one's farm, the only desire was to get away from it and pursue pleasure elsewhere.

SOURCE 16 From an interview with a Suffolk farm labourer, explaining why young soldiers would not become farm labourers

The war had changed the men who had been in the army. They were better educated ... They had a different feeling when they came back. They were not going to do the same things or put up with as much as they did afore they went out.

1. Compare Source 17 with Source 12 on page 7. How has the style of dress changed?
2. Do you think that Sources 15–17 show that life in Britain was 'back to normal'?

Activity

Work in groups.

Take three large pieces of card. The first should have the heading 'Change for the better', the second one should have the heading 'No change', and the third 'Change for the worse'.

Using the information on pages 61–65, fill in each card using words and pictures. Use the finished cards to make a class display.

Was the War a turning point for women?

WOMEN were affected by all the changes we have examined in the last six pages. However, there were some changes which were particularly important for women. We are going to investigate two main issues:
- Did the War change women's jobs?
- Did the War get women the vote?

The right to work

During the War women did jobs that they had not been allowed to do before it. Many of them had reliable well paid employment for the first time. They were paid equal wages to men when they were doing 'men's work'. The money they earned gave their families a higher standard of nutrition and health. It also gave the women greater freedom and more importance in society.

While the War went on the government encouraged them to work outside their homes by introducing measures that made it easier. For example, the government was worried about the way the birth rate was falling. This was partly because women were not keen to have children if there was no one to look after them while they were working. They were also worried about bringing up babies in war conditions and when food was short. In July 1917 a 'National Baby Week' was held to demand better child welfare services. The number of child welfare centres was increased during the War from 350 to 578.

SOURCE 1 Report from the government's medical officers, 1919

66 *Most women enjoyed the more interesting, active and hard jobs, and in many cases their health improved rather than deteriorated. Women have with success undertaken work involving the lifting of weights, heavy machine work, and even forge and foundry work. This shows that light work is not by any means the most suitable for women. The conditions under which women worked before the War, low wages, poor diet, long hours and lack of exercise in the open air, resulted in poor physical health which led everyone to place too low a value on women's strength and capacity.* 99

---

1. How do Sources 1 and 2 differ in their views of women's employment during the War?
2. Can you think of reasons to explain their different viewpoints?

SOURCE 2 From a speech by the Suffragette leader Sylvia Pankhurst after the War

66 *Sometimes women wrote to me, broken down in health by overwork, complaining of long walks over sodden tracks, ankle deep in mud, to newly erected factories; of night shifts spent without even the possibility of getting a drink; of workers obliged to take their meals amidst the dust and fumes of the workshop.* 99

---

3. In your opinion were the changes in women's employment during the War good or bad ones? Explain your answer.

However, after the War, as we have already seen, unemployment was a real problem. One obvious way of solving the problem of unemployment among ex-soldiers was to lay off women factory workers. This is what many employers decided to do. By 1919 around 750,000 women who had factory jobs before Armistice Day had been dismissed. Employers expected that they would simply return to the traditional women's jobs they had done before the War – domestic service, laundry work and dressmaking. Newspapers ran articles such as the one in Source 3 to persuade women to return to their old jobs.

SOURCE 3 From the *Southampton Times*, 1919

66 *Women still have not brought themselves to realise that factory work, with the money paid for it during the War, will not be possible again. Women who left domestic service to enter the factory are now required to return to the pots and pans.* 99

Some women did leave their jobs willingly. Married women with children, whose husbands returned from the War, were generally quite happy to stop work. Some women were not so willing, yet they had no choice, as Source 4 explains.

Munitions workers had often earned nearly £2 per week and they were not willing to go back to earning less than £1.

Source 6 shows what happened to a group of nine women in Southampton. Of these nine only Mrs Brady said she was happy to return to her pre-war job, although Mrs Gregory thought it was only fair to make way for a man.

Some women did keep their jobs, particularly those working in offices and shops, but this sort of work was becoming less popular with men in any case. It seemed that in many ways attitudes to women's work had not been changed by the War. By 1921 the proportion of women who had a job was smaller than it had been before the War, and women's unemployment was a major problem.

SOURCE 5 This young Southampton girl drove a bread delivery van throughout the War, but had to give up when the men came home. She said, 'I cried when I had to come off the [bread] round. I didn't think it was fair; but of course, men were coming home from the War and men wanted jobs. So to see a girl driving round with a pony and cart was not in it'

SOURCE 6 Work done by women in Southampton during and after the War

	War work	After the war
Mrs Stone	farm worker	domestic service
Mrs Bell	Pirelli factory	domestic service
Mrs Gregory	engineer at Avro	domestic service
Mrs Mullins	government mill	nurse on a liner, then left to get married
Mrs Brady	munitions factory	dressmaking
Mrs Kilford	office work	office work
Mrs Barnet	telegraph operator	housewife, looking after child
Mrs Hayes	transport worker	cleaner
Mrs Ottaway	van driver	van driver, but left to get married

SOURCE 7 From the *Liverpool Daily Post*, January 1919

One would think, to hear some people talk, that the whole problem of women's unemployment is to be solved in the near future by a general 'back to the kitchen' movement on the part of ex-munitions workers. Certainly the ordinary man in the street holds that view, but it is not the true one. It is simply a continuation of the old idea that a woman's place is in the home, and if she does not happen to have one of her own, she had best make herself useful in someone else's.

4. Of the newspaper reports in Sources 3, 4 and 7, which take the side of women who wish to work?
5. What reasons might the women in Sources 4, 5 or 6 give for not wishing to return to domestic service or other 'women's' jobs?
6. Why do you think the women in Source 6 who married gave up work?

WAS THE WAR A TURNING POINT FOR WOMEN?

The attitude of many women had changed as a result of the War. Their unwillingness to go into domestic service was seen as a big enough problem for it to be raised in Cabinet. The Cabinet set up a committee to look into the problem. Source 8 gives extracts from its report.

SOURCE 8 A report presented to Parliament in 1919

There is among girls a growing distaste for domestic service under its present conditions and a reluctance on the part of parents to allow them to take up such work . . .

Domestic workers are regarded by other workers as belonging to a lower social status . . . The hours compare unfavourably with any other occupation . . .

As a result the occupation is mainly carried on by unskilled workers who are unable on the one hand to command for themselves satisfactory conditions of employment, or on the other to fulfil their tasks efficiently.

We regard the position as serious in that the best use is not being made of an occupation which might under other conditions . . . be attractive to, and most suitable for, a large section of women workers of the nation.

The committee recommended some important changes to make domestic service a more attractive occupation for working-class women: reduced hours, fixed mealtimes, days off, paid holidays, changed uniform, better food and the introduction of mechanical appliances to help servants do boring and time-consuming jobs. But their report was shelved by the government and no action was taken. It was left for working women either to vote with their feet and leave domestic service, even though many other jobs were closed to them, or to tolerate the low status and poor conditions in order to have some money coming in. The number of women working in domestic service slowly declined after the War although it remained the most common paid work for women for two decades.

However, the government did take more action about job opportunities for educated women. In 1919 it passed the Sex Disqualification Removal Act. This opened up a number of professions to women for the first time. Women could now become barristers, solicitors, auctioneers, surveyors, architects or judges, and could serve on a jury.

---

1. Compare Source 9 with Source 1 on page 8. Has women's employment returned to normal?
2. Look at Source 10. What does it tell you about what a woman's role in the 1920s was seen to be?

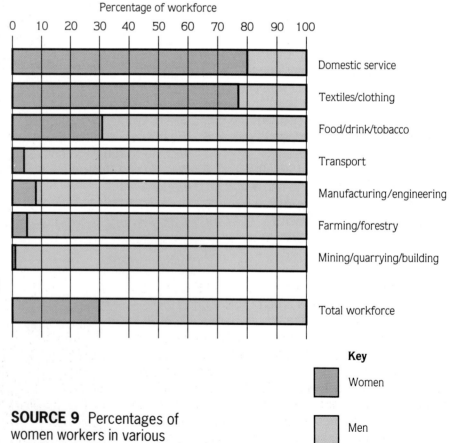

Percentage of workforce

Domestic service
Textiles/clothing
Food/drink/tobacco
Transport
Manufacturing/engineering
Farming/forestry
Mining/quarrying/building

Total workforce

Key
Women
Men

SOURCE 9 Percentages of women workers in various industries in 1931

SOURCE 10 The front cover of the magazine *Woman's World*, 25 June 1927, showing a housewife's weekly work

The right to vote

Before the War, leaders of the Suffragette movement had campaigned quite violently to get women the vote (see pages 10–11). Once the War began, they stopped direct action and threw their energy into the war effort.

During the War there was no General Election. But in 1916 the government decided to set up a committee to plan for the election that would be called as soon as the War was over. The government was worried that under current voting laws most soldiers would not be able to vote, because they had been away from their homes for more than twelve months. The committee was meant to reform voting laws so that members of the armed forces could vote. However, women seized this opportunity to press their demands to be given the vote.

SOURCE 11 Written by Mrs Pankhurst in the magazine *Women's Dreadnought* on 3 June 1916

66 *The forthcoming Bill is supposed to extend the vote to additional numbers of men . . . The Tory press says it will 'give votes to our soldiers and sailors' . . .*

Demonstrations and conferences must be held, petitions organised from every district. The demand must be sent to Parliament that there shall be no half measures . . . but a Franchise Bill to give the vote to every woman and man over 21 . . .

The next few weeks are of vital importance. We must use them in working for Human Suffrage with all the energy we possess. 99

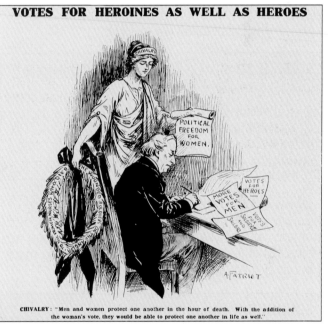

VOTES FOR HEROINES AS WELL AS HEROES

CHIVALRY: "Men and women protect one another in the hour of death. With the addition of the woman's vote, they would be able to protect one another in life as well."

SOURCE 12 A cartoon from the cover of *Votes for Women* magazine, 26 November 1915

Activity

It is 1925. You have been called to give evidence to a committee looking into employment opportunities for women.

What evidence will you give the committee that:
a) the War raised women's expectations of a good job
b) the post-war period has not fulfilled their expectations?

You may wish to refer to pages 54–55.

The conference opened on 12 October 1916. One of the Suffragette leaders, Millicent Fawcett, negotiated with Cabinet officials and an agreement was reached. Women would be given the vote, but – so that women voters would not outnumber men voters – the vote would not be given to *all* women. When the committee made its report it suggested that married women over 30 should be allowed to vote.

David Lloyd George was the new Prime Minister. Before the War his Liberal Party had been split on what to do about women's suffrage. But it was Lloyd George who had asked for Mrs Pankhurst's help in 1915 to get women to work in the munitions factories. He recognised the role women had played in the war effort. In 1917 he put through Parliament a Bill to give women the vote. And so, in December 1917, Parliament gave the vote to six million of Britain's eleven million adult women. There were only 23 votes against. The Bill became law in 1918.

> **SOURCE 13** A speech made by Lloyd George in 1918
>
> 66*It would have been utterly impossible for us to have won the War had it not been for the skill, enthusiasm and industry which the women of this country have thrown into the War.* 99

Many MPs had changed their minds. Before the War, one of the most determined opponents of women's suffrage had been Herbert Asquith, who was Prime Minister until 1916. But by 1917 he had made a public U-turn (see Source 14).

> **SOURCE 14**   A speech made by Asquith in Parliament in 1917
>
> 66*How could we have carried on the War without women? . . . Wherever we turn we see them doing work which three years ago we would have regarded as being exclusively 'men's work'. But what I confess moves me still more in this matter is the problem of what to do when the War is over. The questions will then arise about women's labour and women's functions in the new order of things. I would find it impossible to withhold from women the power and the right of making their voices directly heard.* 99

1. Look at Source 14. Why does Asquith say he has changed his mind about women voting?
2. Why do you think Mrs Pankhurst would be a) pleased, and b) displeased with the new law in 1918? Explain your answer.

Why 1918?

Why did women get the vote in 1918? Was it because the actions of women like the Suffragettes forced the government to give them the right to vote? Or was it because women had shown by the part that they played during the War that they should have the same rights as men?

Below are some of the arguments put forward by historians about why women got the vote in 1918.

1. What do you think? How did each of the following factors help women get the vote in 1918:
   ■ the actions of the Suffragettes
   ■ women's war effort?

The war effort gave ordinary women more confidence in their abilities, and so more confidence in pressing for the vote by political argument.

Suffrage had been extending gradually anyway for the last 100 years. The inclusion of women was bound to come some time. The Suffragette activity and the women's war effort were simply the triggers that helped it to happen in 1918.

1918 and afterwards

The first women candidates stood for Parliament in the 1918 election, and in 1919 women were sitting as MPs in Parliament for the first time. In 1928, all adult women were granted the vote on the same terms as men. Laws were passed that began to improve the situation of women in various areas of their lives. We have already seen how the professions were opened up to women in 1919. In 1923 women gained equal rights to men in divorce proceedings. In 1925 the Civil Service admitted women. In 1930 the Ministry of Health began to make advice on contraception available to women.

1. Write a short essay with the title: 'Was the War a turning point for women?'. Use the information on pages 100–105.

      You will need to consider:
   ■ what the situation of women – both poor and rich – was before the War
   ■ how their situation changed during the War
   ■ how their situation changed after the War.
      Then draw some conclusions about whether the War was a turning point.

You have now studied what Britain was like before the War, during the War and after the War. You are going to create a wall display called 'Changing Britain'.

1. Look back at pages 4–11. Use words and pictures to show how Britain after the War was different from Britain before it.
2. Working in groups, decide which of these changes a) would have happened even without the War, b) happened because of the War.
3. On your own, write three paragraphs to explain whether you think the War made Britain a better place to live.

Without the violent campaign the Suffragettes fought before the War, no one would ever have taken their cause seriously and the government would have kept on postponing a decision, thinking that it was not an important issue. The Suffragette campaign was proof that women wanted the vote, and wanted it enough to go to prison for it.

The violence of the Suffragettes actually held back women's suffrage because it lost them the popular support they had. They could have had the vote much earlier than 1918. Their violent campaigns made the government more determined not to give in.

Prior to the War many men did not see women as capable. But the women's war effort changed forever the way many men saw women and they could no longer support an electoral system that excluded them from voting.

What was the impact of the War on Europe?

YOU have already studied the impact of the War on Britain (pages 95–105). In many other countries in Europe problems were similar or worse.

Death and destruction

Millions of young men had been killed and even more had been wounded and maimed (see Source 1). Some soldiers who suffered the effects of shellshock never recovered for the rest of their lives. Others found it hard to return to the routine of civilian life.

Many women who had been widowed by the War had to support their families on their own.

In Germany some people were close to starvation.

In certain areas close to the front line, there was ruin and destruction (see Source 2). Homeless people had to be resettled and houses rebuilt.

As if these problems were not enough, Europe was hit by a devastating flu epidemic from 1918–20 (see page 95). Soldiers and civilians, weakened by hunger and exhaustion, had no resistance. It is estimated that 20 million people died of flu, many more than had been killed in the fighting throughout the whole of the War.

SOURCE 1 It is not known exactly how many soldiers died. The table below shows the estimated number of dead and wounded for each country

	killed	wounded
Germany	1,900,000	4,250,000
Russia	1,700,000	4,950,000
France	1,400,000	2,500,000
Austria–Hungary	1,300,000	3,620,000
Britain and Empire	998,000	2,300,000
Italy	615,000	947,000
Turkey	350,000	450,000
Romania	340,000	510,000
Bulgaria	95,000	155,000
Serbia	50,000	134,000
Belgium	44,000	45,000
Portugal	7,500	14,000
Greece	5,500	9,000
Montenegro	3,500	6,000

▶ **SOURCE 2** The Belgian town of Ypres close to the front line, had been home to thousands of people in 1914. In 1918 it was a ruined ghost town

Debt and depression

Europe was deeply in debt. Many countries owed the USA enormous sums of money which they had borrowed to pay for war materials. European industries were geared to war production and it would take time to change back to producing peacetime products. There was no money to buy goods from other countries. World trade slumped. The slump meant that there was high unemployment and returning soldiers found it difficult to get jobs.

Bitterness and blame

There was a legacy of bitterness throughout Europe. The French blamed Germany for starting the War. They felt extremely bitter about the destruction caused in northern France and about their war dead. They wanted to make Germany pay. Many British people felt the same. They wanted to bring Germany to its knees and protect their own interests.

Many Germans did not believe they had lost the War. They had simply agreed to an armistice. They felt betrayed by their rulers, and angry towards Britain and France who seemed to want Germany to accept all the blame for starting the War.

SOURCE 3 Cartoon, British Empire Union, 1919

Political chaos

The Great War created political chaos in many countries. It marked the end of the three great empires which had dominated the European mainland. Europe was in a state of turmoil – old governments had gone but stable new systems had not yet had time to be set up.

■ The War had helped to bring about a revolution in Russia. The Russian Empire had been replaced by the communist Soviet Union.

■ The Kaiser had fled from Germany. The German Empire had been replaced by a new but very unstable democratic government.

■ the Austro–Hungarian Empire had disintegrated. If you think back to the beginning of this book, on pages 12–15, you will remember the role of Serbian nationalists in triggering the start of the War. With the collapse of the Austro–Hungarian Empire, the Czechs, Slovaks, Serbians, Croatians and other Slav peoples had their wish for independence, but this did not mean they they were content. Now they were arguing among themselves as each national group tried to get as much territory as it could for its people.

Activity

The Versailles Peace Conference
In this atmosphere, leaders of the victorious countries met at the Versailles Peace Conference in 1919 to agree terms for peace. They all wanted to ensure that such a war could never happen again, but they had very different ideas about how to achieve it.

1. Imagine you are attending this conference. You have been asked to prepare three proposals which you think will help prevent another war. List your three proposals as bullet points and explain why each one will help. Later in your course when you study the Treaty of Versailles you will be able to compare your ideas with decisions taken at the actual conference.

2. Explain in your own words why it was going to be difficult at the Peace Conference to reach a settlement that would prevent a war happening in the future?

Investigating the First World War

THERE is evidence about the First World War all around us. Its memory is still with us today in the poppy symbol worn on Remembrance Day. In many family histories there are memories of casualties.

Let's see how you might investigate the casualties in a local area.

We are in Ringmer, a small Sussex village. The war memorial lists 42 names, but some of them are not very clear.

Inside the church is a roll of honour which also lists the names.

Some of the dead are buried here. This is what a serviceman's gravestone looks like.

So we have our names. Can we find out more about the people? In the local library I'm looking for documentary evidence. The local newspaper is on microfilm in Brighton Library. I start with the Battle of the Somme, as it's more than likely that some local people died there. Ah, yes... there are details of how and where two of them died.

The library also has a copy of a directory which lists all the property holders in Ringmer in 1913. It gives me addresses and occupations for some of the people on my lists.

I've come to visit the relatives of some of the soldiers. Anyone who was alive during the War is very old now. Will they remember anything? Perhaps they may even have diaries, letters, postcards or photographs from the time...

I remember when my uncle came home from France, my Mum had to use a hot iron to get rid of the lice in his clothes... and I remember that the lad from the Post Office — Frank Wilmshurst — he got killed. He was a great friend of my uncle.